Hello,
My Name Is
Single

What others are saying. . .

This book looks at those who walk, work, and worship among us, often unseen, sometimes pitied, and usually misunderstood: single Christians. *HELLO, My Name Is Single* is witty, engaging and, above all, completely honest. In other words, it isn't the Christian version of *Sex in the City*. Adriane doesn't present single life as all *Cosmo* and care-free dating, with a little Jesus thrown in. Rather, she presents singleness as a cross-centered struggle with the self and with God. She treats singleness as a station in life, a godly vocation that may or may not be permanent. The book's core message: Don't panic, don't give up, don't give in.
—*Todd Wilken, host of Issues, Etc.*

Adriane sets out a worldview confirming any life worth living begins in the recognition that there exists an enduring moral order, and that there is a certain greatness in humility and service. Her vantage point is crystalline, and she has given us a narrative that is eloquent, lucid, timely, and more relevant than ever to our time and our culture.
—*Tim Goeglein, Senior Advisor to the President & Vice President, External Relations, Focus on the Family*

Heins's perspective and humor about single life is a welcome read. Heins addresses it all, from dating discouragements to temptations, offering a candid and biblically informed read that takes on the needs and questions of today's singles. Not only for singles, there are insights for pastors, and the book encourages single souls (and those who love them) to expect blessing!
—*Dr. Beverly Yahnke, Professor of Psychology, Chair of Social Sciences Department, Concordia University Wisconsin*

Backed by research, experience, and a keen eye for culture, Heins deftly chides, counsels, and encourages both singles and those around them, always anchoring the discussion and the hope of all in their identity as those redeemed by Christ.
—*Pastor Tim Pauls, Good Shepherd Lutheran Church, Boise, Idaho Author of* You Ask About...Relationships *(CPH 2007), Going Out, Getting Dumped and Playing Mini-Golf on the First Date (CPH 2005; now out of print)*

Honest. Frank. Witty. Necessary. This book is a high-octane treatment of a long neglected topic.

—*Rev. Marcus Zill, Full-Time Campus Pastor & LCMS Coordinator for Campus Ministry (LCMS U)*

Adriane Heins has written a complex book on a pretty complex subject.

Truth is, not everyone will agree with Adriane's conclusions. Some, in light of today's cultural norms, will take issue with her. But she stands true to what she believes. There is no doubt this book could stimulate spirited conversation. Given the mores and values of today's world, it's a conversation that needs to happen.

—*Dr. Terry Dittmer, Director of LCMS Youth Ministry, member of the Association of Youth Ministry Educators and Religious Conference Management Association, author, editor, composer*

Adriane Heins has done us all a big favor in writing *Hello, My Name Is Single*. Adriane pulls no punches, taking on the unique joys and heartaches of the single life with both humor and pathos. Candidly and personally, she reveals the many social, sexual, and spiritual implications of the single life. Get your copy today; you'll be all the richer for it.

—*Rev. Harold L. Senkbeil, STM, DD Executive Director for Spiritual Care DOXOLOGY: The Lutheran Center for Spiritual Care and Counsel*

This is a book that pretends to be about singles, but it is really about the suffering and hope of all Christians who live in a broken world and are waiting for the life to come. Rather than devolving into pandering, moralistic lectures, she centers all of her advice, which is aptly, humorously, and plentifully illustrated with examples from her own life, upon the resurrection of Jesus Christ. I don't care who you are: read this book.

—*Rev. David H. Petersen, Redeemer Lutheran Church, Fort Wayne, Indiana*

Adriane Heins pours out her heart about her experiences and the plight of many who are single. I especially enjoyed her thoughtful treatment on the Church Fathers and Martin Luther on important topics that singles should be considering in this day and age. This is a thoughtful book for young singles and those who are young at heart.

—*Rev. Craig Donofrio, Pastor, former dating coach, author of* Attraction, the Christian Man's Dating Guide *and radio host on Worldwide KFUO radio*

I love this little book. From the first sentence, Adriane surveys the issue of living as a single adult more honestly than any other book on the subject, but with a sensitivity that breathes hope. And the book is hardly just for singles. It's packed with information on this 44% of the population of the U.S., a demographic of people who are all about us, who love us, whom we love, and with whom we interact—often without much sensitivity to the challenges they bear and the gifts they bring. I love the author's constant play on pop themes, pop tunes, and pop psych as she deconstructs the myths of singlehood, absent a blathering pseudo-spirituality but filled with deep Christian piety. "It's a small wonder our Lord doesn't finally let loose with His own Frasier/Niles moment, yelling, 'Copernicas just called, and you are not the center of the universe!'"
—*Matthew C. Harrison*
   President, The Lutheran Church—Missouri Synod
   Assistant Pastor, Village Lutheran Church, Ladue, Missouri

This book can help to restore that calling of singleness in all of the challenges of contemporary life. Adriane Heins writes with wit, honesty, and wisdom. Her book will prove to be a lifeline to single Christians.
—*Gene Edward Veith, author of* Spirituality of the Cross *(CPH 2010) and* Family Vocation *(Crossway 2012)*

Unflinchingly honest and surprisingly hilarious, *Hello, My Name Is Single* is a helpful and encouraging book—not just for people who are single but for their friends and family as well. Finally, a book that acknowledges the reality and complexity of single life while avoiding meaningless platitudes or false promise. Adriane Heins writes with vulnerability, intelligence, humor, and joy—all with the aim of helping single people trust that God loves them.
—*Mollie Hemingway, Senior Editor at* The Federalist

Hello
My Name
Is

Single

How I Learned to Ignore the
World's Expectations and Trust God

Adriane Dorr Heins

Concordia Publishing House

3558 S. Jefferson Avenue

St. Louis, MO 63118-3968

1-800-325-3040 · www.cph.org

Text © 2014 Adriane Dorr Heins

Library of Congress Cataloging-in-Publication Data

Heins, Adriane Dorr.
  Hello, my name is Single / Adriane Dorr Heins.
    pages cm
  Includes bibliographical references and index.
  ISBN 978-0-7586-4199-1 (alk. paper)
  1. Single people--Religious life. 2. Single people--Conduct of life. I. Title.

BV4596.S5H45 2014
248.8'4--dc23

2014008486

1 2 3 4 5 6 7 8 9 10   23 22 21 20 19 18 17 16 15 14

Contents

✳✳

To you who are single, that you would find contentment in Christ, who is and remains your only comfort and hope, and who reminds you daily that "I am with you always, to the end of the age" (Matthew 28:20).

✳✳
Introduction

You're single. You've been single. You met a single person once. You've dumped people, and you've been dumped by people. You've known great loneliness and worry and sadness. You've looked at couples, married or dating, and been jealous. You've wanted what they have, what the Lord has chosen not to give you right now. You've prayed. You've stopped caring. You've given up. You've tried harder. And some days, most days, you've wondered why, despite your cries to the Lord, He seems so silent. Your name—your very identity—hinges on a word: *single.*

All of that, all of those emotions you experience oh-so-acutely, are normal. It's all right to feel them. We all deal with our single-ness differently, and sometimes we choose not to deal with it at all. Throughout this book, you will do both: understanding better what it means to be and live as a single man or woman in this world while simultaneously realizing that the Lord's plan for you may be very different than the one you imagined for yourself. You may feel vindicated; you may grieve. You may pray harder and worry less. Whatever the outcome, you will know, by the time you turn the final page, that the one who created this world—its pine trees and sea horses and penne pasta and you—loves you and that you are not alone. You won't find *Cosmo*'s "Three Reasons Being Single Is So Fabulous" in the following pages. You're not going to hear tips on how to spiff up your online profile so that you'll be more attractive to the opposite sex. You're not even going to have to decide if you should call yourself "single," which implies an inherent aloneness, or "unmarried," which presumes that your last step to being a complete human being is to dredge up the next breathing member of the opposite sex and swap rings.

I'm not even going to tell you that being single is fun and exciting, because a lot of days, it's not. I'm also not going to promise you that the Lord has someone in mind for you, because I don't know that either. Marriage, as we all know too keenly, is not meant for everyone.

But in this book, we will strive at all costs to be honest with one another. Here, you don't have to put on a brave front. You don't have to act like being single doesn't matter to you or that it doesn't find its way into your thoughts twenty times a day. For now, you get to just be who you are: single and suffering, single and content, single and wondering, single and alive. You get to be mad or sad or frustrated or happy or content or free. Reading this, you get to do what you want.

No matter how you feel about the Lord's will for your life right now, whether you're simply surviving being single or whether you hate every minute or whether you relish your independence, this book will help you to realize who you are. And if being single is painful to you, it will help you realize that eventually, the pain of not having a pious spouse will lessen. Maybe it will ease because the Lord will provide you with a godly husband or wife. Maybe it will be because He will teach you to be content in your singleness.

> You are loved. You are not alone.

Through it all, you will endure. Even more, you will carry on in hope because, as my pastor reminds me, "God really is good and He does work all things, even really painful things, together for good. We live by faith, not by sight, in spite of the evidence, and we wait on the Lord. And that, of course, is the definition of hope." You will recognize the burden for what it is, and it will no longer define you.

That's the point of all this: You have hope, and that hope has a name, and the name is attached to a flesh-and-blood man, and He is Jesus. Look to Him, to the one who was nailed to a rough cross, bloodied and gasping for breath. Look to that Jesus, the one who knows your aloneness better than you know it yourself. Look to Him, to the one who endured the ridicule of the crowd, the torture of His captors, the taunts of the devil. Look to Jesus, who cried out in words you have sobbed too: "My God, My God, why have You forsaken Me?" (Matthew 27:46).

He is your Jesus: He was broken, wounded, hurt, and suffering. He felt and experienced all of that for you, on your behalf. He suffered all that so that you—in your rawest, messiest moments and just as much in your contented, happy ones—may always have the assurance that He has taken whatever you may feel about your singleness onto Himself.

Just as He shoulders that weight, so always He heaps on you blessing upon blessing. He is your Jesus: risen from the dead and triumphant over your loneliness, shame, and discontent. He is present with compassion, with a peace so tangible and powerful that you can't fathom or understand it, with love that assures you that you aren't alone.

This Jesus—on the cross and outside the tomb, in the Word and in, with, and under the bread and wine delivered into your mouth on Sunday morning—feels what it means to be single more intensely than you do. He rejoices when you rejoice, and He mourns with you when you mourn. But He is yours, and you are His. And because He lives, because no feeling or emotion has any hold on Him, you live too, and those same feelings and emotions find their rest, their relief, in Him. When you are scared of being dumped, He promises never to leave you, even though your girlfriend might. When you fear your heart can't take any more rejection, He promises never to hurt you, even though your ex-husband did. And when you worry that you will never meet someone, that you will go through this life all by yourself, He promises to be with you always, even if He chooses never to give you that spouse.

You are loved. You are not alone. You are not defined by being single. No, you are a child of God: whole and perfect, broken no more.

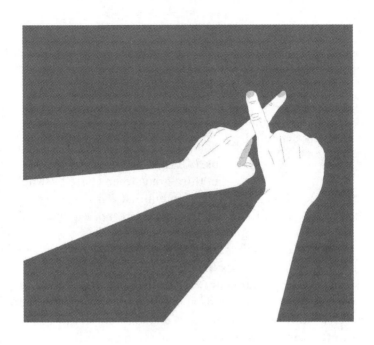

Chapter 1

The Untouchables

It was the first Sunday after I started my new job. I was in a new town looking for a new church with a new pastor. As a single person, I was hoping to find a congregation like the one I'd just left: one where members ate meals together in the church basement on Christmas Day and families were so close that children sat with other parents on Sunday morning in Bible class. But this Sunday, sitting alone in a new space, I felt an odd affinity with the lepers who cried out to Jesus in the Bible—untouchable and unloved. I couldn't shake the sense that the woman down the pew was giving me the stink eye, and I was confident that the usher in the back of the church had raised his eyebrow at me in a less-than-charitable fashion on my way in. Even if neither were true, I was experiencing what most singles feel all too routinely: we convince ourselves that all the sideway glances and hushed voices are directed toward

us. It doesn't matter if we've been married and are widowed, have
never had a boyfriend or girlfriend, are divorced, or are simply not
looking for a relationship. In the church and in the world, we feel
different from everyone else. We feel isolated, unlovable.

> In the church and in the
> world, we feel different
> from everyone else.

We shouldn't. It's not like we're sick
or falling apart. We're not diseased.
You can't catch anything from hugging
us. (All right, so there was that time
in third grade when I gave my whole
Sunday School class the chicken pox, but that was *not my fault!*)
We don't live in colonies, set apart from the rest of the "normal"
population.

No, single people are just people, with a set of lungs and a heart
and a brain just like couples in relationships. And single Christians are baptized children of God, just like married Christians.
But while we know in our heads and wish in our hearts that there
weren't such differences between us and everyone else, we notice
that divergence most particularly—and often painfully—within the
church.

It makes sense when the world gives us the hairy eyeball. After
all, we expect the culture to treat us differently as Christian singles. We know we're in opposition to much of what it stands for and
how it defines what relationships are and should be. We don't buy
into the lie of the random hookup, and we're well aware to be on
alert for temptation, mindful that pornography is available with a
click or two on the Web. We're prepared to do battle with those who
would seek to devalue the worth of marriage and children, and
we're fully cognizant of the fact that these beliefs may be the cause
of suffering for the sake of Christ on our part. But in our churches,
in our congregations, we expect to feel accepted. We want—desperately—to fit in.

It's frustrating when we don't, especially because we're aware
of our differences in a socially awkward sort of way. We sit alone
in the pew. We kneel for Holy Communion by ourselves. We pray
alone. We even sit by ourselves in Bible class. Not that we want to.
We want to be loved as a part of our church's family, to feel just
as valued as the couple with the two wild daughters pulling their
dresses over their heads while wriggling around under the pew at

the early service. Stronger still is the growing feeling that we're the problem, that something's actually wrong with *us*. We convince ourselves that we're not normal, that we're deficient in some way, that we're not good enough to be a part of the Body of Christ. We don't have children, so we have no one to take to Sunday School. We have no husband to help tear down tables after a potluck, no wife to drop off a pot of soup for the new mom who's resting up at home. We can't help with Vacation Bible School because we're at work, and we can't make the weekly Bible study because it's at 10 a.m., right in the middle of our work day. And so we start to think that the gifts and talents we have to offer the church are very small indeed—and when no one tells us otherwise, we actually start to believe it.

We want—desperately—to fit in.

❋❋

Burdens upon Burdens

Beyond feeling set apart, we're also easily worn out. Being single can be exhausting, and it's especially so for women. We were created and designed to be cared for and about. So when there's no one there to watch out for us, no one to make sure that we are safe and all right, when we are the ones who have to be our own guardians, we're done in. Something as simple as keeping track of all the bills and the grocery list and the next doctor's appointment and when insurance is due requires feats of strength tantamount to the fist-clenching power of the Hulk. There's no one to talk to about the weird ka-chunking noise the car is making; no one to bounce ideas off of about the annual Christmas card; no one to say, "You stay put, and I'll pop a bag of popcorn—don't leave the couch." Instead, we are resigned to calling our fathers or brothers, mothers and best friends, admitting to them that we're out of our league and that, once again, we need help. Suddenly, we've forgotten that our Lord gives blessings upon blessings. Now it simply feels like burdens upon burdens.

While I feel keenly the plight of single women, single guys don't have it any easier. They're made to defend women and children, to care for those whom the Lord has entrusted to them. But it's hard to care for people who don't yet exist and harder still to have the energy even to want to, when women today don't seem to want that kind of care in the first place. Not to mention the fact that there's no warm house to come home to, no dinner to enjoy with a woman anxious to listen, no beautiful girl to go shopping for Christmas presents with. Life—it seems—is reduced to beer and pretzels, football games, and being the third wheel. And who wants that?

It's why meeting another single person—male or female—feels like such a relief. "Here's someone who understands! Here's someone who knows! This person can commiserate. She'll understand me." We are like two Texans meeting up in the middle of Kansas. (Have you ever noticed how excited Texans get over meeting other Texans? I mean, really: it's a little over the top.) We gravitate toward our own kind, toward people who are also alone.

In an instant, we form a connection. We share stories of failed relationships and frustrations and mutual hopes for the future. Among women, there's a fair amount of male bashing, and men share knowing winks and elbows to the ribs. But male or female, we take comfort in simply knowing another single, in knowing that we're not alone, in knowing that someone else out there gets us.

All of these feelings combine into a swirly, deadly concoction of worry, isolation, and exhaustion. The devil uses it to his advantage. He loves this trio. He comes to you in your weakest moment, when you are tired and alone, and asks you, "Why are you worried? Didn't God promise never to leave you or forsake you? Then why do you feel like He has? Is it because, just maybe, He actually *has* ditched you?" He whispers, "I get it. You're alone and feeling miserable. It stinks. But, hey, you're alone—which means nobody has to know if you take a peek at that porn site. Oh, come on. It's just between you and your Internet provider. You'll feel better afterward. I promise." He tempts you with "It's been a long day. You must be wiped out. I thought Jesus told you to take His yoke because it was light and you would find rest. You don't seem like you've gotten much rest to me. Is He leading you on?" His whispers work, and we believe him. Alone with our thoughts, we find it easy to fall into disbelief, not taking our Lord at His Word that He alone has met all our needs on the cross.

The devil is tireless. He never stops planting the seeds of lies and half-truths, fear and doubt, so thick that they grow quickly to be tangled jungles of sin and death. And yet that mass of overgrown evil is the very thing that our Lord slashes down, hacking away and cutting down all our transgressions, all our doubts. He clears the path and makes the way straight. He tells us again that we are His and that we are safe: "My sheep hear My voice, and I know them, and they follow Me. I give them eternal life, and they will never perish, and no one will snatch them out of My hand" (John 10:27-28).

THE FORGOTTEN ONES

Our Lord sets the standard—the high bar—for how we as the Church are to care for those among us who are single. We realize by the way in which He shows love that a connection shouldn't be formed just between singles—or Texans—but that pastors and grandmas and uncles and children ought to reach out to the singles among us in the same way. He causes us to realize that too often, we in the Church have failed to love our single neighbors. We have failed to care for them in a manner that points everyone with whom we come into contact to Him and to His gifts of mercy and, ultimately, of peace.

We spend a lot of time talking about the importance of marriage in the church. We teach about the gifts that are to be had in marriage, about the way in which our Lord created Eve for Adam, about the joy that comes from serving a spouse. Bible-study participants discuss the top ten ways to have a better marriage, and moms meet at church with their toddlers to discuss among themselves how children ought to be raised in homes with both a mom and a dad, and why those relationships are at the very core and backbone of our society. We have marriage retreats, and we order special after-service cakes for couples whose anniversaries fall on Sundays.

As singles, we get it. We support those conversations and actions and all they entail. And just as much as we can appreciate their value, we simultaneously loathe them with a burning sort of hatred that's largely unhelpful and probably verging on psychotic. We love them just as we hate them. They remind us of what we long for. They give us hope that perhaps, one day, the Lord will place us

> We are under the burden of being single.

into families of our own. They teach us what godly marriages look like and how men and women are made to interact with one another. And we despise them because they make it all too clear that we are under the burden of being single, that what we want is not ours, that those around us have been given what we don't have.

We see these things lived out in our church families, and especially each Sunday. We are reminded of the way in which our Lord designed men to give themselves to and serve women, and the way in which women are made to receive the care of men. We watch each week in church at the way in which the Lord relates to His people, how He remains the Church's faithful Head. We take great joy and comfort in knowing that we as the Church are His pure and chaste Bride. Through it all, we learn how men interact with women by watching the way in which the Lord interacts with His people. We watch. We pray. We hope.

Nevertheless, we leave unsettled, sighing to ourselves as we walk to our car, certain the church has forgotten to talk about us—the singles. More important, we worry that she has forgotten to talk *to* us. We are the forgotten ones. The church takes pity on the widows, and she remembers the orphans. Church members have the elderly into their homes, and they invite the youth group over for dinner. But the singles are forgotten. Or worse still, they're often simply overlooked. And so the feeling of isolation, of being different and misunderstood, continues to grow, even among those who ought to care most for us.

Pastor Christopher Seifferlein, in a letter to his congregation, acknowledged that the church goes to great lengths to remember and celebrate weddings and anniversaries, but it rushes right past those who have no spouse.

> *Do we have more to say to the widows, the unmarried, and the divorced than that their best years are either behind them, or else that the most they can hope for is someday to meet "Prince Charming?" Are single people second-class citizens . . . like people on the outside looking in?*

It may appear that in the church that we also present these false ideas. We have weddings in the church, but no special celebration for single people. There are flowers on the altar for those celebrating wedding anniversaries, but I have never seen flowers on the altar for someone celebrating their singleness. Imagine the bulletin: "The flowers today on the altar are for Ms. Jennifer Smith, who is thanking God for her 25 years of singleness." Even in his preaching, the pastor may use examples from married life. This, of course, is expected, as he is married, but the question may be asked: With all this talk about marriage, does the Bible have anything to say about the state of singleness?[1]

Waiting with Them

The church can and ought to mend this gaping wound. Christ has shown us how and has equipped His Church to be the best suited to dive into the gray of loneliness with the black-and-white clarity of His Gospel. We have been—indeed, we are—living in a pregnant moment.

We, the church's members, can love those among us who have no spouse to love them in return. We can invite them to sit with us at church, call to check in with them, drop them a note now and then, and remind them of their value and worth. We can give voice to the single person's unique and individual vocation, his or her God-given place in this life, the means through which God uses that person to serve those with whom he or she comes into contact. Some of the singles among us are aunts and sisters, uncles and brothers. They are editors and teachers and farmers. They are Sunday School teachers and elders, ushers and organists. They are family and friends. They are employees and co-workers. They do it all. Still, many of them pray that they might be given one more vocation: that of husband or wife. And while they wait, we wait too, reminding them of the place and plan God is using for them and on their behalf right now.

We can listen too. It's not easy; our tendency is to fill the silence. We want to offer advice: "Have you tried online dating?" "Maybe you're looking too hard." "Have you thought about getting into a singles Bible study?" But sometimes—most times—our single brothers and sisters don't need advice. They've already heard it all, and they know it by heart. Instead, they just want to be heard. They need to know someone cares. They need to know they matter, that their opinion is valid. They need to be validated.

> We can give voice to the single person's unique and individual vocation.

Even more than all this—more than understanding that they feel out of place, more than listening, more than dredging up, yet once more, feelings of loneliness—we can point them again and again to Christ. We can remind them of Him who puts the solitary into families, who loves the singles as much as He loves those who are married, who looks and sees a baptized child of God, who holds back nothing simply because of a relationship status.

This is, as Rev. Matthew C. Harrison said, our "fundamental gift and task":

> *To bear witness to Jesus Christ—to His Gospel and all its facets (AC VII 2; FC EP X 7). This is our task toward each other. This is our task over against those who do not know Jesus. This is also the sacred vocation and ecumenical task of the Missouri Synod to world Christianity. We exist to bear witness—even to the point of suffering and death (and it may well come to that sooner than later here in the West)—to salvation by grace alone, through faith alone, on account of Christ alone. This Gospel is God's own testimony about Himself. This is the very confession of Christ Himself. This is the witness of the apostolic Church and the Church of all ages. This is the witness sealed by the blood of Jesus, the blood of John the Baptizer, and the burning of John and Henry, confessed and sung by Luther.*[2]

This is our charge as the church: to our single brothers and sisters, to those who are married, to the widowed, and to those whom the Lord has blessed with celibacy. If we never invite them to dinner or never ask them to join our small group, if we never help to lift the burdens they bear and the pain they feel, if there is only one thing we do, let us be privileged to point them to Christ, no matter the cost. As we do, may we learn together, as the Body of Christ, that we are not so different from one another after all. Baptized into Him, we are one, and suddenly we are no longer alone.

Leave Us Alone

We can blame ourselves—in part—for how we feel. We foster a culture of aloneness. In fact, we're exceptionally good at being alone. We are alone with our computers, alone with our thoughts, alone with our headphones and iPhones, alone with ourselves.

Family meals are no longer a priority. Moms take kids to church while dads go golfing. We blog instead of chatting; we text instead of talking. We go to dinner with friends and look at Facebook while waiting for our meal to arrive. We text our roommates instead of talking to them, and we play video games instead of going to baseball games. (Don't believe me? Read Robert Putnam's *Bowling Alone*.)

In truth, we don't underhandedly foster solitude. We're downright bold about it! At lunch with my family one day, my brother-in-law, a pastor, noticed a couple sitting at an adjoining table. They were young and obviously waiting on their food. She looked bored; he was studying his phone. She stared at the wall, while he stared at a screen. It was a sharp and dismal contrast: two people, together, but each of them most definitely, obviously, alone.

My brother-in-law, who was wearing his clerical collar, got up from his chair and went to the table. He put his hand on the young man's shoulder. "Are you two related?" he asked.

The young man was startled. "No," he stammered. "I mean, yes. She's my wife."

"That's what I figured," my brother-in-law smiled. "You should probably put your phone down and talk to her."

The woman looked relieved and smiled ever so slightly that someone was advocating on her behalf.

"She's beautiful," my brother-in-law said. "Chat with her. Ask her about her day. This is a good thing, I promise you."

He patted the stunned man on the shoulder as he walked away. "Have a good day, you two."

It was something to behold: we have become a culture that must be told to interact with other humans.

The singles among us know differently. If there's one thing we *don't* want, it's to be alone. We're downright sick of it. Tired of it. Totally and completely over it. You wouldn't know it to look at us. From all outward appearances, singles look fine. (We won't, by the way, be wearing a scarlet letter S on our jackets, so you'll have to look hard to spot us. We're tricky that way.) We don't have kids to pick up from T-ball practice or spouses to fuss with. We don't seem sad or depressed. We have jobs and lives. We go to parties and crack jokes and laugh off our singleness when people bring it up. (And they do! Boy, do they.) And so our church families assume we aren't suffering.

> Baptized into Him, we are one, and suddenly we are no longer alone.

Indeed, perhaps not all singles are. Perhaps some are given to singleness for the entirety of their lives. Perhaps some are simply waiting and praying. Perhaps they are doing the only thing they can do: clinging to those promises of God, holding the Lord to His own words that it is not good for man to be alone, praying for peace.

That's why it's a bit funny that we as Christians fuss and fret about mission work, anxious to support those who take the Gospel to the ends of the earth (and that, I might add, is good; that is the church at work), when we as singles are proof that there is much the church at home can be doing as well. If ever there were a mission field begging to be harvested—let us be clear—we are it! One-third of America's population is single. That's 102 out of 314 million people, many of whom are alone, frustrated, anxious to be in community, and eager to be loved.[3]

They are among us in our churches, beside us on the street, behind us at restaurants, and in front of us at red lights. They are in jobs, out of jobs, and looking for jobs, in our cities and in our rural and small towns. In their twenties and thirties—the years during which they ought to be at the height of marrying, having children, buying homes, settling down, and maturing—a majority of both men women simply aren't. Instead, they are and continue to be alone.

Today, the numbers are more striking: 23.8 percent of men, and 19 percent of women, between the ages of 35 and 44 have never been married. Tick back a cohort to the people between 20 and 34—the prime-childbearing years—and the numbers are even more startling: 67 percent of men and 57 percent of women in that group have never been married. When you total it all up, over half of the voting-age population in America—and 40 percent of the people who actually showed up to vote this time around [2012]—are single. . . . How did we get to an America where half of the adult population isn't married and somewhere between 10 percent and 15 percent of the population don't get married for the first time until they're approaching retirement?[4]

The number of singles on the rise doesn't impact just the singles themselves. It has an effect on how our society functions, what families and congregations look like, the growth or decline of different kinds of religions, what kinds of things we place value on in this world, and how we exist as a culture. The theological implications of a nation at ease with and in support of such high levels of unmarried people affects the culture, and the way in which the separation of sex from marriage and family has further eroded the desire to be married and in a family ought to be explored. As the church, our confession about what it means to be alone and what it means to be put in a family—in a marriage—means something. We do not stay silent when the world around us derides the biblical understanding of marriage, claiming that it is an institution based on the feelings of adults alone. We speak up when others would have us say that "what's true for us isn't necessarily true for them." We voice our support of marriage as God designed it: for one man and one woman. We are in a time that demands "the mind and the spine," as Dr. William Weinrich, a professor of church history, told me.

Comfort and Care

The Church's moment is now. Its moment always has been, and always will be, now. There is an enduring need for us as Christians to bear witness to Christ to those who do not know His comfort and His love. There is a profound need to show mercy to these singles who need our consolation and our care. And there is an opportunity to experience and enjoy a robust life together with a group that is desperate to be a part of something outside of themselves.

Even as we are reaching out and toward those outside the church, we must also wrap our arms around those already taking part in our congregations and Bible studies, those within our families and our circles of friends, those Christians already in the Body of Christ who struggle with being single. They are hurting, and they are in our midst. We as the church can and must bear their burden with them.

> We must also wrap our arms around those within our families and our circles of friends who struggle with being single.

That's why it's so heartening that you—single and alone or married and concerned—are willing to engage in this discussion, to speak about and be open about what it means to be single. You as a Christian can help the church of today learn that it's all right to engage in a conversation with those who are praying for and waiting for a spouse; that it's all right for those who are married, who are living and rejoicing in a Christ-centered Christian marriage, to offer comfort to the singles among us.

You're the ones who can help others understand what it means to be single, what to look for in a spouse, and what things to pray for in that regard. This conversation not only provides a platform for those in the church who are single to share their suffering but it also gives those who are married a chance to see the blessings of singleness that will be theirs one day in heaven. You are the ones who set the standard for what the contentedness of a Christian marriage can look like. You are the ones who give us hope that Christ will bless us too, even as we tell ourselves that there is no hope for people like us.

So whether you're married or single, engaged or widowed, had fourteen boyfriends or no girlfriends, at the end of the day, you are a part of what it means to be the church: that we bear one another's burdens and frustrations; that we are sinners in need of our Savior's forgiveness; that we learn from and with one another; that when one of us suffers, we all suffer; and that we rejoice in the hope, the forgiveness, and the wholeness that is ours in Christ.

To you who are single, know that this hope and joy aren't the kinds of hope and joy that you get from opening a Christmas present to find the latest tablet device, or those thirty seconds of awesomeness when you find five dollars in the jeans you washed last week. This hope and joy come from Christ. They are His gift to you, to see you through all the blessings and challenges of living the single life. The joy isn't a momentary, fleeting kind of excitement. It's an enduring comfort, one that He gives you fully and constantly, the comfort that will see you through the lonely nights and the frustrating mornings, the good days and the hard ones. It is His joy, molded and shaped perfectly to fit exactly what you need, and it is all for you.

MARTIN LUTHER: SECOND SUNDAY AFTER EPIPHANY

The highest and most significant point of this Gospel [John 2:1–11] is that we must give God the glory of being kind and gracious, even if He Himself acts and speaks differently, and all our mind and perception think differently. In that way our perception is killed and the old man perishes, so that only faith in God's kindness remains, and no perception remains in us. Here you see how [Jesus'] mother retains an untroubled faith and holds it out as an example for us. She is certain that He will be gracious, though she does not perceive it. It is also certain that she perceives differently than she believes. For that reason she lets it be free and committed to His kindness, and determines for Him neither time nor place, neither manner nor measure, neither person nor name. He will do it when it pleases Him. If it does not happen during the banquet, then at the end or after the banquet. [She thinks:] "I will swallow this slap down: that He treats me with contempt and leaves me standing in disgrace before all the guests and speaks so unkindly to me, so that we all blush for shame. I know that He acts bitterly, but He is sweet." Let us do the same, if we are true Christians.

(*Church Postils II*, Luther's Works 76:244)

Chapter 2

How Do I Live?

The church spends a lot of time talking about families and marriage and love. These are, after all, the ideals that Christ sets before us. He loves us, His Church, and in loving us, He gives couples the perfect pattern for the way in which they ought to love each other. But what does He have to say about the single person, the unmarried one who doesn't have someone to love him or her in the way that members of a couple love each other?

Scripture, despite how it may feel to us, isn't silent on this matter. The Lord has something to say specifically to you, to all of us who are single. In fact, He's given several passages of His Word over to the understanding of the single life, words meant directly and specifically for the comfort and assurance of those who have no spouse. And that's a lot of us! Forty-four percent of Americans are single,[1] which ought to be profoundly comforting for all of us included in that number. After all, there's only one of us, and there's 100 million of them, which means that finding a spouse shouldn't theoretically be all that difficult, right? Hello?

> Forty-four percent of Americans are single.

True, 100 million singles gives you more than a handful of options. (Just remember what your grandma told you: "There are plenty of fish in the sea." I don't actually know what that means, but at least remember that she told you.) But what are you supposed to be looking for in a prospective mate? And what kinds of qualities are negotiable? Can you handle a girl who sneezes with all the tenacity of a hairy trucker for the rest of your life? Does your future husband *have* to be a Christian?

Singles today, unlike our parents and grandparents, don't have the benefit of having solid marriages and shining examples of singledom to look up to. It's increasingly rare that parents stay married and together and in the same house and in love for life, that our peers grew up in loving two-parent homes, that the ideas of what it means to be male and female were discussions around the dinner table. Looking beyond our parents' relationship, our culture doesn't offer much help in this regard either. (Cue Kim Kardashian, for example, who was still married to Chris Humphries while pregnant with Kanye West's baby. I'm going to need a flow chart to follow what just happened there.)

Consider, if you aren't already whistling the tune, the words of Irving Berlin's infamous song "Anything You Can Do." When you get past the incessant bickering in the song ("No!" "Yes!" "No!" "Yes!" Gah! Stop arguing already. I mean, what does *that* say about how the culture views relationships?), you get a clear view of the world's understanding of gender. The American culture we inhabit promotes a woman that is just as good as a man, or even better. In fact, she doesn't even need a man! She can adopt kids, break through the glass ceiling, write a book, start a charity, walk the dog, blog, get her nails done, head up the PTA, and do it all in heels and without a man's help. And as for you men, well, the culture wants you to live in perpetual high school, eyeing a different girl's body every night, failing to open doors for her, dodging responsibility, playing beer pong until you're forty, and not feeling the least bit ashamed of it, all with a video game controller in your hand.

That's what our culture would have you do. That's the yellow-brick road it wants you to follow, and more than that, it really wants you to believe that that's the best way to live your life. It really, truly wants you to buy into that idea that no one else—nothing else—matters but you. Your behavior, your friends, the way in which you carry yourself, your future, even how you treat others all pale in comparison to what makes you feel happy right now in this moment. The world shoves the First Commandment to the side, encouraging us to most certainly have other gods and really just one god in particular: ourselves. It's a small wonder our Lord doesn't finally let loose with His own Frasier/Niles moment, yelling, "Copernicus just called, and you are not the center of the universe!"

"At Last, My Love Has Come Along": Sing It, Etta

Instead, God bids us turn to the One who does matter. "Lord," we finally sigh in exasperation, "to whom shall we go? You have the words of eternal life" (John 6:68). Scripture tells us who has the answers to our struggle against putting ourselves before God and our neighbor. And—spoiler alert—it's not the marketing campaign the world is selling. In Genesis 2, our Lord reminds us that it is not good for man to be alone. And it's not just any kind of alone. Adam had plenty of company: elephants and apples, paradise and the Lord who walked with him in it. But the Lord said Adam needed a special kind of company, one unique to man. He needed a person to take care of and to love (and in our day, someone to keep us from putting ourselves first!). That's why He created woman, to be a suitable helper for man, bone of his bone and flesh of his flesh. And how does Adam respond? "Then the man said, 'This *at last* is bone of my bones and flesh of my flesh" (Genesis 2:23, emphasis added).

He says, "At last." Finally. All is as it should be.

That "at last" is what the single person waits for, the relieved sigh he longs to exhale. It is the "at last" that closes the door on flying solo and opens it up to the institution explained in Genesis 1, that which begins and ends with God, sandwiched with what it means to be male and female in between. "God created man in His own image, in the image of God He created him; male and female He created them" (Genesis 1:27). It is the "at last" that mirrors Christ's own love for His Bride, His Church, the tangible relationship explained in Ephesians 5: "Let each one of you love his wife as himself, and let the wife see that she respects her husband" (v. 33).

That "at last" is what brings us full circle: back to us who are single, to those who appear to be the exceptions to the rule in the kingdom of God and the norm in the kingdom of the world.

However, we have a golden ticket that culture can't give us: we are not alone, and we don't live as though we are. We are one with Christ, even if we have no spouse or boyfriend or girlfriend or any friends at all, and He is the one who gives us our value, our worth, our meaning.

As Christians, we know well our biblical history and the Scriptures that have spoken of those to whom God did not give a spouse. Consider the woman at the well (John 4) who knew her share of marriages, divorces, single- ness, and more marriage. Or think on Daniel, John the Baptist, Anna, Paul, Moses' sister Miriam, Elijah, Mary Magdalene, Lazarus, the Ethiopian eu- nuch—and *Jesus*. They were all single.

> We are not alone, and we don't live as though we are.

Paul tells us that singleness is a "gift from God" in 1 Corin- thians 7, a divine gift, and yet simultaneously one that can be an intense burden to those who are in Christ. In that vocation of sin- gleness, Paul says, a person can devote himself more fully and pro- foundly to our Lord's work, which, while noble, comes with its own unique set of blessings and challenges. Some people, our Lord says, are even born specifically for such a life, uniquely suited to live in such a way that many—even the majority—cannot. "For there are eunuchs who have been so from birth, and there are eunuchs who have been made eunuchs by men, and there are eunuchs who have made themselves eunuchs for the sake of the kingdom of heaven. Let the one who is able to receive this receive it" (Matthew 19:12). To live a life of celibacy is its own gift and challenge, acknowl- edged in these words by Christ Himself, and those who are blessed with the gift of celibacy are rare. "If chastity were possible to all, it would not require a peculiar gift," the Lutheran Confessions ex- plain. "But Christ shows that it needs a peculiar gift. Therefore, not everyone has it" (Apology of the Augsburg Confession XXIII 19). (In this day and age, even those who are still virgins are rare!)

Chastity Revisited

Sexual desire is God's gift to mankind by which He intends to join two opposites as one flesh and from their union to create still other people in His image and likeness (Genesis 2:24). Yet ever since the fall, every God-given gift is susceptible to hijacking by devil, world, and flesh. Thus God-pleasing sexual desire turns into lust, hunger becomes gluttony, ambition morphs into pride—you get the picture. In each case, something God gave humanity for the benefit of His children becomes first self-gratification, then obsession, and finally idolatry. Yet in Holy Baptism, Christians are both buried with Jesus and raised with Him (Romans 6:4) so that they are no longer slaves to sinful passion. Dead to sin and alive to God, they are called to offer their bodies (yes, those parts too) as living sacrifices, holy and acceptable to Him (Romans 12:1). Daily, they put off their old sinful nature and "put on the Lord Jesus Christ" (Romans 13:14) so that their whole body together with its desires may be used for God's glory and the neighbor's benefit instead of selfish gratification.

"Chastity" may sound strangely antique to our ears, but that's the virtue Christians over the centuries (even eras as decadent and sexually charged as ours) have cultivated to direct the powerful force of sexuality for good. Chastity means abstinence apart from marriage and faithfulness within it. It's framed within the fidelity of the heavenly Bridegroom and His earthly Bride, the Church. Living no longer for themselves but for Him who died for them and rose again, godly men and women find fulfillment using their desires not for self-indulgence but for the benefit of others and the God who made, redeemed, and sanctified them as His own.

Chastity means you're not less of a man or woman if you're not active sexually as an unmarried person. Chastity means you let your spouse's needs and desires supersede yours if you're married—and yes, at times, that means abstinence for a while. You may be out of step in a sex-crazed world, but you are a citizen of another Kingdom that transcends

this world. Thank God, He forgives and restores every penitent sinner through faith in Jesus Christ, His Son, and by the cleansing, enlivening power of His Spirit. A chaste and decent life is therefore not oppressive but is fulfilling for all those who live by faith in God and by love for their neighbor.
—Dr. Harold L. Senkbeil, Executive Director for Spiritual Care, DOXOLOGY: The Lutheran Center for Spiritual Care and Counsel

To the man or woman who is single but not celibate—that is, who still prays in earnest that he or she might be placed into a marriage pleasing to God—Scripture has words of encouragement: "Be free from anxieties. The unmarried man is anxious about the things of the Lord, how to please the Lord" (1 Corinthians 7:32). As singles, we don't often think of this because, quite honestly, we're too caught up in worrying about our own hurts and frustrations. But it's something we ought to meditate on: as much as it may hurt to hear it, not having a family really does free us up as single men or women to spend more time in the Word, to help the single mom in your congregation by watching her kids so that she can run to get groceries, to bake brownies to take to mid-week Bible study, to talk to your pastor about what doesn't make sense, to go out to the Cheesecake Factory with a friend who needs someone simply to listen and offer counsel, to pick up an extra shift when someone at work needs to leave early, to drop to your knees in prayer that our Lord would stretch and grow your faith like a taffy puller on steroids. Conversely, those who have spouses or perhaps families find their time divided between work, school, and children. On top of that, they have to make time for one another and for church, not to mention getting groceries. And who's picking up the dry cleaning?

He Loves the Unlovable

The time and ability to serve the Body of Christ is one of our best and most needed gifts as singles. The devil tempts us to think that we are the only ones with troubles or that marriage would solve all our problems. But it's actually the opposite! For this reason, Paul says, "To the unmarried and the widows I say that it is good for them to remain single as I am" (1 Corinthians 7:8), for "those who marry will have worldly troubles, and I would spare you that" (v. 7:28). To our single ears, that doesn't sound like much of a comfort. "Give us the worldly troubles," we volunteer. "We'll take them! Gladly!" Instead, Scripture bids us not only to cast those cares on the Lord but also to come alongside of others who experience suffering and to help them shoulder the load, "[bearing] one another's burdens" (Galatians 6:2). We do this not because we have to or because it wins us invisible brownie points with God. We do this because it is one of the ways in which the Lord uniquely uses His single children in service to His Church.

And so it all boils down to this: All of us—single or married—want to place our importance and our worth on something we can control, rather than find it in Christ. We want something that's not ours to have (at least not yet), and so our Good Shepherd responds to us in a way that teaches us again what His good and perfect will for us is. He draws us back to Himself, prodding us gently with His staff, a reminder that He knows what is best for us and that His plans for us are for our "welfare and not for evil, to give [us] a future and a hope" (Jeremiah 29:11). In this, our Lord reminds us that "We are justified neither because of virginity nor because of marriage," but instead that we are redeemed "freely for Christ's sake, when we believe that for His sake God is merciful to us" (Apology of the Augsburg Confession XXIII 36).

This is how Christ acts in mercy toward us: He puts us in a community, in His Church, and entrusts us with holy things, with His work to do. When we fail miserably, when we put ourselves in front of others, He forgives. When He moves us to care and love one another, He rejoices. Consider the Book of Hosea as an example. (If you are not yet married, read this book to learn what repentance, faithfulness, and an enduring ability to forgive look like. If you are married, read this book to learn better how to love and forgive your spouse.) In Hosea 2:19–20, the Lord says to His people, to His Church: "I will betroth you to Me forever. I will betroth you to Me in righteousness and in justice, in steadfast love and in mercy. I will betroth you to Me in faithfulness." This is the way in which the Lord cares for all of His children—regardless of their marital status. He is the Bridegroom. We, as His Church, are His Bride. The perfect husband, Christ, loves us even though we are unlovable and forgives us even when we don't want to be forgiven. He, "your Maker," "is your husband, the Lord of hosts is His name," Isaiah says (54:5).

He cares for us as a husband cares for his wife, putting protective measures in place for those of us who are single to keep us from hurting ourselves and from being hurt. He puts boundaries up for those who are married, that they may find joy and not pain in one another. He is the Bridegroom to His Bride, the Church, teaching us what it means to live by faith, causing us to trust that He means what He says when He says it, relying only on Him and not on our relationships or lack thereof. He gives us His Word, filled with comfort regarding the joys of the single life and the fullness of the Gospel meant for those who wait on Him with hope and patience.

Scripture has much to say to those who are married, but there is joy to be found in this: we have a Bridegroom, and He is Christ. Like a compassionate husband caring for his wife, He does not leave us to suffer in silence, nor does He refuse to grant us a word of peace. Instead, He gives His grace—vibrant, whole, and tangible—to all of us, married or single. Better still, it is undeserved! He gives it to the virgin and the celibate, the married and the widow.

> *Just as a public speaker is not more righteous before*
> *God because of his ability to speak than an architect*
> *because of his skill in architecture, so a virgin does*
> *not merit justification by virginity any more than*
> *a married person merits it by conjugal duties.*
> *Each person should faithfully serve in his own gift*
> *and believe that for Christ's sake he receives the*
> *forgiveness of sins and through faith is regarded*
> *righteous before God.*
> (Apology of the Augsburg Confession XXIII 39)

In this way, He does something else that is really quite remarkable: He does what a husband would do for his wife. He eliminates that sense that all of us singles dread, the feeling that sets us apart and makes us different from everybody else. By loving those of us who are single just as He loves those who are married, He un-sets us apart. No longer are we the lepers, the outcasts, the ones who get the raised eyebrow because we don't have what our siblings and friends and co-workers have.

In this normalizing, He forgives our sins. He washes away each sin

> No longer are we the lepers, the outcasts, the ones who get the raised eyebrow.

of lust caused by a simple glance at the woman walking down the street, of envy over the third engagement we've seen on Facebook this week, of doubt that He actually knows what He's doing when it comes to us. In that forgiveness, He reminds us again of our place in His kingdom as His Bride. He puts us, the solitary, in the midst of His family. He tells us of heaven, of His mansion prepared for us, a place in which we will never again know loneliness. And suddenly, we are not so different anymore.

You Could Generalize, but You'd Be Wrong

I am most frustrated when people assume that I am single because I want to be single. They assume that I don't want to be tied down, don't want the extra work, or am not interested in marriage. In reality, I strongly desire to be a husband and a father; I just haven't been able to find someone who I feel comfortable filling the other half of those roles. I'm frustrated when people lump me in with the mindset of the American male as popularized on television, in the movies, and by the media.

I don't want to sleep around; I don't want to live alone; I don't want to wait for marriage until our culture says it's appropriate; I don't want to live in a man cave, eat ramen noodles, and play video games. I do want responsibility; I do want commitment; I do want a faithful, godly, beautiful wife; I do want kids; I do want to love and care for one woman for the rest of my life. Call me crazy, but don't assume that I want to avoid marriage as long as possible. Living life as a single man, you slowly discover areas of single life that just don't quite cut it, because while leaving your clothes in the dryer for weeks at a time and eating an entire jar of peanut butter for supper may seem like glorious liberties to the casual observer, the glamour leaves pretty quickly. One begins to realize that there's something missing. Someone, rather. Sometimes it just takes a few weeks, sometimes a few years, but eventually you come to the realization that it is indeed not good for man to be alone: (1) When the workload and pressure at your job keep building and you feel like you're running in place; and all you want is to be able to lay in bed at night with your wife and tell her about it, to rest for a moment and let down your defenses. (2) When you've just finished fixing something around the house, and no one is there to be super impressed with your semi-mediocre, halfway-reasonable, not-all-that-great-but-I'm-still-learning-and-I-did-it-myself repair. (3) When you're tired of your meals stinking;. (4) When you're tired of sitting alone in church and driving home alone afterward. (5) When you get tired of the way our culture treats boys and girls and want to raise your girls to be beautiful, modest women and let your boys play in the dirt and grow up to be strong, faithful men. (6) When you want to love a wife . . .

Somewhere in there, you realize that it is not good for you to be alone. But somewhere in there you also learn that in the end, your trust is best placed in God. It was He who created you, He who atoned for you with His own blood, He who sustains you. He knows your needs, and He does not abandon you. It doesn't always happen on your time or in the way that you'd like it to, but even so, that trust is still best placed in Him. In whom else would you place it?
—Sam, late twenties

Chapter 3

Potato, Potahto

Almost all of us have been to weddings during which the pastor read Matthew 19:4-6: "Have you not read that He who created them from the beginning made them male and female, and said, 'Therefore a man shall leave his father and his mother and hold fast to his wife, and the two shall become one flesh'? So they are no longer two but one flesh. What therefore God has joined together, let not man separate." And almost all of us who are single have dreamily wondered if that joining together might one day be for us. (Well, after we've finished sobbing into our ripped-up tissue, that is.)

That "holding fast," the "clinging to" of a husband to his wife in emotional, spiritual, and even physical ways, especially in the New Testament, appears to the norm. So if man isn't supposed to be alone but is, and if a woman is made to be a helper, but has no one to help, where does that leave them? Where does it leave us? And what does the Church say that healthy relationships between a man and a woman should look like?

Designed and fitted to live under Christ's cross, we know that while the world and even certain denominations within the Church Militant tell us there are no underlying differences between the sexes, well, we know differently. Beyond the physical and emotional differences between men and women, beyond the amount of shopping done by the one and the cold pizza consumption by the other, there's one fact that cannot be ignored, one that actually gives form and shape to what it means to be a single Christian praying for a godly spouse. That one thing? Our Lord became incarnate as a male.

It doesn't seem to be all that important, right? Male, female; potato, potahto. But the gender in which Christ enfleshed Himself has a lot to say about what it means to be a man, and from that, plenty about what it means to be a woman. Once we know what it means to be a man and a woman, we'll have a better understanding of how the Lord desires those two to fit together. So let's look to Jesus and His person and work for a few minutes to give us a glimpse into the implications of a God who specifically chose being a man as the way in which He would reveal Himself.

Making a list of Christ's qualities bears witness to who He is as a *man*. His gender is not incidental to our salvation, to His relationship to us. It shows us that He maintains the very structure—the order—He gave us in creation in the first place, that all of that giving that He does is very intentionally done for us. It proves that the way in which He revealed Himself wasn't haphazard or by accident. Everything that Jesus does and says teaches. So, let's see what He has to tell us about what our genders are designed uniquely to do.

Step 1: Put justification, Christ's atonement for the sins of the world, at the top of the list. As a male, Jesus was humbled by taking on Himself "the iniquity of us all" (Isaiah 53:6). As a male, He sacrificed His life so that others might live. As a male, He became responsible for the sins of the whole world.

As a male, He advocates for sinners before the Father and reconciles them. As a male, He sits at His Father's right hand and acts on His behalf. As a male, He has overcome sin, put death to death, and unseated Satan and his angels.

As a male, He instructed those around Him: teaching, preaching, and baptizing. He gave them His Word, His truth. As a male, He has made clear the profound Word of God and opened to us, His children, a vault of heavenly words and churchly language.

As a male, He gives the faithful His Sacraments. He offers up His male body, flesh and blood, to eat and drink. He gives pardon and peace, strength and preservation until the Christian is brought to rest and eternal life.

In and by each of these actions, Christ remains in a continual posture of giving. He gives of Himself, gives His forgiveness, gives His Father's gifts of mercy and grace, and finally gives His own life. As a male, He is categorized by what He gives, what He does, how He acts. Each of those acts—those gifts—are holy, pious, and perfect.

He gives all of this for the benefit, the protection, and the strengthening of those who receive. They are those things that defend Christians against the devil, help them resist temptations, and allow them to stare death unflinchingly in the eye. They offer comfort and consolation, show compassion to the suffering, and come alongside a world broken by sin.

Those things that make Christ who He is—and who He is uniquely as a male, as a giver—are necessary for the perpetuation and vitality of the Church, and they are necessary for you men who desire to be godly boyfriends and, one day, husbands. They are equally necessary for you women looking for a Christian man whom you can love and serve alongside one day. Understanding why Christ is a male, and what that means for men, gives the Church form and shape, provides order in the midst of a world in chaos, and helps you understand what life under the cross as a baptized man of God really means.

Men Give; Women Receive

Now it's the ladies' turn. With Christ's maleness as our model, we as the Church look to other examples of the proper relationship between male and female. We see that most clearly in the very order of creation God established in the Garden of Eden and in Adam's subsequent reflection of Christ's maleness.

Adam gives to Eve: his rib, his affection, his completeness. He gives protection, a home, love, contentment. He shares his actual, tangible paradise with her, and together they walk with the God who created it. Adam provides her with food, with companionship, with no need to feel or be ashamed, even with a name: "Woman, because she was taken out of Man" (Genesis 2:23).

Eve receives, and she rejoices. Her femaleness reacts in kind to Adam's maleness. She responds by collecting all that he has to offer, and all that he offers is exactly what she needs. He fulfills her desires, meets all her demands, leaves her wanting nothing. He truly does complete her. Her response is pure and chaste love, utter unselfishness, and resplendent joy.

Thus the relationship of giver to receiver begins to pattern itself, flowing naturally to the relationship of husband to wife. Like Adam, the generations of men who followed him are in the business of giving. Husbands protect their wives, offer them guidance, ensure that they have sustenance and warmth, and see that they are about the things of God and in His house.

Dr. Gene Edward Veith describes the way in which Christ would have these one-man-one-woman relationships work:

> *So how did Christ love the church? By harsh domination? By forcing the church to wait on His every whim? No. "Though He was in the form of God" He "made Himself nothing, taking on the form of a servant" (Philippians 2:6–7). He gave Himself up, "to the point of death, even death on a cross" (2:8), out of love for His church.*
>
> *That is how a husband is called to love his wife, denying himself for her sake. This rules out every kind of selfish demand, every authoritarianism, much less cruelty and abuse, with husbands instead emulating the self-sacrificial love of Christ. When a wife feels loved like that, it is much easier for her to submit to a husband whom she knows is giving himself up for her.*
>
> *In this dynamic relationship of submission and self-sacrifice, there is no room for power-plays or manipulation or tests, just each partner serving the other, putting the other first.[1]*

But with the entrance of sin into the world, things that Adam did not have to give Eve must now be given to women by men. Now they must offer their fidelity, faithfulness, truthfulness, and their word. Even the perpetuation of their lineage and design of their bodies manifest their creation as giver.

Like Eve, wives receive, and they rejoice in what they have been given. They submit in an anxious desire to embrace that which their husbands have sacrificed to give them. But this "subjection [is] not compelled through a demand or by force." Instead, it is a reaction, a response, to their husband's maleness, an "insight into God's order of things."[2]

To submit to her husband means that a wife responds in faith, trusting that what her husband has given her is good and true, that he means what he says when he says it, and that his gifts are those that are best and right for her.

"As the husband cannot attain to the ideal of Christ's love without self-denial, so the wife cannot conform to the ideal of the Church's love to Christ without surrender of self to Christ's precious will."[3] And so the woman, the wife, submits, not as one who no longer has a voice or an opinion, but as one who is open to receiving all of the best of what her husband has to give. She "learn[s] quietly with all submissiveness" (1 Timothy 2:11). That is to say, her response is one of humble gratefulness, modesty, self-control.

What It Looks (or Should Look) Like

Men give; women receive. So it is with the relationship of Christ to His Church on earth, that perfect union of our Lord and His Bride. That's wonderful news! It means that the way in which God gives to you and the gifts you receive from Him, that pattern and model, is the very way in which you can practice what it means to be in a healthy, robust, God-pleasing marriage now—before you're married, before you go out on a first date, before you sign up for eHarmony. Sunday morning affords you the opportunity to learn what it means to be a husband and what it means to be a wife, and it's all in one place, in one hour, in the Divine Service, in church.

> Men give; women receive.

There, as "in all ages, God remains the gracious Giver, while we [the church] always remain the recipients. God is always the eternal Initiator. We receive the gifts He chooses to bestow."[4] In fact, "The church has existed since the Garden of Eden. Adam was the first pastor. Eve was the first congregation."[5]

That is to say, the Lord gives His body and blood, His Word, eternal life, access to the Father, forgiveness, and peace. And the Church—the woman—receives, and she rejoices. She is the faithful, the redeemed, those who live in and by Christ's death on the cross, His ultimate and best gift.

We as the Church are humble and not proud. We do not demand the spotlight, nor do we look for recognition. Instead, we are "willing to receive His self-denying service, even to the point of death, and then in turn being appropriately responsible to the one who has graciously taken the responsibility for [her] protection and fulfillment."[6]

Just as a wife does not make outrageous demands of her husband, so the Church does not attempt to bully Christ into getting what she wants. "The Church is obedient to the call of Christ's love while enjoying the liberty with which Christ made it free. . . . It does not want to rule Christ but wants to be ruled by Him, while expressing in prayer its desires and resting to be heard."[7]

So, what began with Christ's maleness in His incarnation, and was witnessed in the first man and woman ever created, continues today through the vocation of marriage, but it can also be seen and understood in the Church and her relationship with her Lord.

The order of creation—that is, the relationship of giver to receiver—finds its basis in Scripture and in Christ Himself. It is His order, His design, given by His own Word in creation.

This, then, is how God made men to interact with women, givers to receivers; this is how He designed them to complement each other, how He intended them to exist in His creation. Therefore, as singles, practicing our relationships with the opposite sex in the way Christ interacts with His Bride, the Church, we can be assured that such a relationship, if He chooses to bless us with one, will be founded in and by Him and will be holy, pleasing, and—Goldilocks-style—*just* right.

What This Means for You Dudes

If men are to give and women are to receive, and if the relationship between the two is really nothing more than a reminder of and refocusing on the way in which men and women were created and the unique paradigm into which they fall, why all the fuss?

One option stands out as the most viable: that in those passages (such as 1 Corinthians 14) that say women are to submit and men are to lead, women are to be silent and men are to show the way, it is not the women who are being called to account, but the men.

Consider the account of the fall in Genesis 3. The devil targets Eve. She is the more fragile of the two humans, the weaker vessel. This is not because she does not have the same mental capacity as Adam or is less valuable. Instead, Adam is stronger in that he is the one to whom the Lord gave His command: "You may surely eat of every tree of the garden, but of the tree of the knowledge of good and evil you shall not eat, for in the day that you eat of it you shall surely die" (Genesis 2:16-17).

This leaves Eve exposed, vulnerable. She did not have the benefit of hearing what Adam heard; she had not yet been created. Thus, it was Adam's job—as male, as husband, as giver—to share that word with her, to provide her with what she could not have known on her own, to give her what she needed to protect herself from the attacks of the devil. It was his duty to give her Christ's gifts, indeed, to be Christ for her. Eve had no one but Adam for this. She needed what he had to give. Her life depended on it.

That is why the devil targets the female. That is why he tempts her with what may have been a holy-sounding gift. Perhaps that is why Eve is caught so unaware. She is drawn in because the devil has something to give her: the promise of knowledge on par with God. And in her piety, Eve responded in the way in which she was created: ever ready to receive.

In that moment, Adam failed his wife. He did not give her what he promised: his protection, his paradise, an unadulterated and pure relationship with God. Instead, he left her to experience "the height of folly . . . to crave that which the Lord has not given her."[8]

That is why, when He walks in the garden in the cool of the day, "God called to the man" (Genesis 3:9). It is Adam to whom He poses the question "Have you eaten of the tree of which I commanded you not to eat?" (v. 11). It is Adam of whom He demands an answer: "Who told you that you were naked?" (v. 11).

It is Adam who has disobeyed. It is Adam who has fallen down on the job. It is Adam who is ultimately held responsible.

Adam. The man. The giver.

Although Eve sinned first, "It is Adam who is confronted by God as having ultimate responsibility for the fatal rebellion" against Him.[9] Adam refused to do what his maleness required, and Eve's femaleness suffered the consequences.

Perhaps, then, the answer to the questions of what women can and cannot do, especially when it comes to how we live as singles in the Church, is answered best by what men should and ought to be doing. Perhaps it is that 1 Corinthians 14 is not, in fact, a condemnation of women but instead a reminder for the men of the Church to return to the substance of which they were created: giving the good gifts of God to women eager to receive them.

Perhaps passages such as 1 Corinthians 14 do not, as the world claims, mean Christ is unfriendly to women, that He created them as inferior beings, that they are not smart enough, wise enough, pious enough to lead.

Perhaps it means simply that God created men and women for a specific order and that order is meant for the benefit and well-being of each sex.

Perhaps the men, following Christ's lead, are there to give only the best to women, and the women, in turn, are there to receive them with grateful and humble joy.

Perhaps, then, it means it's time for you men to reclaim your maleness.

That's right. I said it.

What I mean is that men are often unwilling to be in the mode of giving, because giving is hard work. It takes initiative. In order to give something, you have to have something to give in the first place. And doing the hard work of getting something to give means sacrifice and effort.

This lack of willingness for men to be truly male is part of what got us into this feminist mess in the first place. Men weren't stepping up in their churches and their homes. Things were sliding. They weren't doing what God had given them to do. They were, as we all are, being lazy and selfish.

> It is time for you men to reclaim your maleness.

So women decided that if men weren't going to step up to the plate, the ladies would just do it themselves. And they did. (Even though the proper response would have been to encourage the men in their lives.) And then, rather than stopping the women in their tracks and saying, "No, that's not yours to do. That's actually my job, and I apologize that I've failed to do it," the men sat back, cracked open a beer, and let the women lead. *#fail*

It's time that you men relearned what it means to be a man, what it means to be a giver. That is what you are uniquely suited to do, and it's time you get back to the business of doing it. Paul demands it. He says, "Saddle up, boys. It's time to ride."

Well, not really. He actually says, "Be watchful, stand firm in the faith, *act like men*, be strong" (1 Corinthians 16:13, emphasis added). You get the gist.

That's what has to happen. Men have to reclaim their role in churches. They have to reclaim their role in the home. They have to reclaim their role as spiritual heads of their households.

All that reclaiming means a whole lot of work. But in so doing, through prayer and repentance and God's grace, you men will find that women, when they begin to see this transformation, just may in fact learn to step aside and actually let you really *give,* as males were created to.

What This Means for You Ladies

This doesn't mean women are off the hook. It means we relearn to trust our pastors, our fathers, our boyfriends. It means we spend an awful lot of time in prayer and repentance. It means we begin slowly to realize our rightful place as receiver.

That will be difficult to do. I guarantee it. It will feel weird and wrong, like we're giving up something that's ours to have. The culture will get in our way. Our pride and our egos will make us want to flee back to our old ways, the ones where we were in charge and got to order the men around. Our stubbornness and our desire for independence trip us up.

Nevertheless, God is faithful. He doesn't just sit back and watch these relationships implode like a science project gone awry. (Not that I would know what that looks like or anything. By the way, sorry, Unity Christian High. I hope that lab is working again.) He sends faithful pastors and dedicated laymen into our midst, mothers and fathers and sisters and brothers, teachers and friends and mentors and books, to help distinguish between these two unique, very virtuous roles.

Moreover, we can—yes, we ought—to pray. That's primary, because spending time in prayer, by virtue of the very nature of the act, returns us as women to a posture of reception. It teaches us again how to receive the mercy that the Lord gives in His gift of prayer. Then there are all sorts of things beyond that: We repent. We live in forgiveness. We support the men in our lives: our fathers and brothers and boyfriends, if we have them. We love our neighbor. We seek out the company of women who are mature in the faith, and we learn from them.

Through all of this, we begin to learn again the uniqueness of our femininity. We recognize the difficulty of being a male and realize that it is not for us. We see that it is ours not to lead but to support, to receive, to come alongside, to nurture.

It is good for us as women to spend time in prayer, in God's Word, and at the Lord's Supper because those are the gifts, given us by Christ and by our pastor, that will teach us again what it means to receive, and thereby, what it means to be female.

As you do, take comfort in this: In Christ, we are all one, whether married or single, widowed or divorced. We are all mothers, all sisters, all daughters, all friends. We are not alone. We are a part of our Church and its family. As one pastor wrote:

> *I have fond memories of my father distributing roses to all the women in the church on Mother's Day back in Trinity Church in Flatbush . . . making no distinction between those who were mothers and those who had no children, some of whom, indeed, had never been married. . . . In distributing flowers to all the women on Mother's Day, my father was acting in accord with the teaching of the gospels that the church brought a new reality in which our relationships as mothers, sons, daughters, sisters, and brothers really have little or nothing to do with our original family relationships. In the church all women who have heard the word of God and kept it are mothers and sisters of Christ.*[10]

This is a long, wordy way of saying that when we discuss what it means to be a man and what it means to be a woman, it's not simply a discussion of "no" and "you can't" and "Go fish." Instead, it's a biblical road map to understanding what God designed each sex uniquely to do.

Jesus Was Single Too

So what does it mean to be a Christian man? What does being a Christian woman entail? This distinction is important, because it's often easy for those without a spouse to struggle as they try to find and determine their purpose. The quest for finding meaning is time-less; it can plague us from the moment we wake up to the silence in which we fall asleep at night. The Lord created us to be in commu-nity, to serve one another in love, to submit as women and to lead as men. When there is no one to submit to or no one to care for, no community to be in and no one to serve and love, it can leave us feel-ing empty.

When we feel empty, we feel alone. And feeling alone is, hands-down, the one feeling a single person knows all too well. When this feeling is coupled with actually being alone, we find it easy to feel that we have no value and no worth if we don't have a spouse or chil-dren. We find ourselves angry and confused, unsure of why it feels like we were created to be and do something that we can't. That's when it becomes commonplace to blame the Lord for telling us it's not good to be alone but then not setting us in homes and families.

While we may not understand in this life why our Lord has chosen to withhold, perhaps only for a time, the blessing of marriage, we can know this: Christ gives us worth, and He provides us with a purpose. In Him, we aren't alone, and we don't need to be self-reliant.

Our meaning in this world as a single person is ours in Christ by virtue of His death on the cross. When His Father looks at us, He sees His Son, broken and yet triumphant, humbled as He overcomes the world. Christ and His cross are our reason for being. They give us our meaning. Not in archaic, dusty ways, in the kind that allows us to think, "Sure, He understood people's problems *then*. But can He really understand what I'm experiencing *now*?"

> **Christ gives us worth.**

He can. He does. He was, after all, a single man Himself. He knew loneliness. (How do you say "Garden of Gethsemane" in Aramaic?) He knew what it meant not to fit in and not to have a place. (Remember that line about birds and foxes?) He knew what it meant to rely on others. (Consider His mother, John, and others.)

Our Lord understands more acutely than any of us what it means to be single, what it means to be truly alone. His disciples abandoned Him. His own hometown rejected Him. He was tempted by Satan himself. Despite all this, He's also the one who willingly took on all the gunk and sin and slime and dirt of the world. And He did it alone.

He's also the one who was raised from the dead, the one the grave couldn't hold, so that you don't have to be alone. He's the one who joins you to Himself in the watery pools of Baptism, so that you are always someone's, always His. He's the one who places you into a family, a community, His Church. He's the one who promises never to leave you, never to forsake you (Hebrews 13:5).

He knows your loneliness. He understands your fears. He hears your worries. And He answers, because you matter to Him.

Perhaps that's at the root of loneliness: feeling as though you don't matter. If there is no one to check up on you and no one for you to check up on; if it feels like no one needs you or maybe you don't need anyone. If what you do or where you go is completely up to you, it feels like nothing you do matters.

This just in: you matter. Thinking that you don't is an evil, nasty trick of Satan's. How he must cackle with glee when the saints of the Lord think that their lives aren't worth much because they have no one with whom to share them! How he must roar in delight at the thought of God's children shedding tears or losing sleep over their loneliness. (And if he taps the tips of his fingers together like the Grinch while he's at it, that wouldn't surprise us a bit either.)

So remember this: you matter. You are a person, flesh and blood, made of the same stuff and substance as our dear Lord, Jesus Christ. He became as you are because you matter to Him. He felt loneliness, abandonment, freedom, and joy just like you do, because you matter to Him.

If you needed a cherry on top, get this: you matter to the Father too, because you matter to Jesus. You matter because nothing would deter Him from offering up His Son's life so that you wouldn't have to suffer and so that you wouldn't have to suffer alone.

You have value. You have worth. You do because you are Christ's. You are somebody's, and He is yours. No one can snatch you from Him. You aren't alone. You have a Father who created you, a Savior who saved you, a Holy Spirit who intercedes and prays on your behalf. You are blessed indeed!

All of this is yours. It's a blessing, a gift, given freely and received joyfully. It's yours. It's the Lord's. (And, unlike the Broncos jersey your ex-girlfriend gave you, there are no strings attached.)

It's further proof that singles do indeed have a purpose, and that our purpose is to bear witness to Christ and His gifts, whether there's a wedding band on our ring finger or not. "There is neither Jew nor Greek, there is neither slave nor free, there is no male and female, for you are all one in Christ Jesus" (Galatians 3:28). (And yes, we can easily add "single or married, widowed or divorced, celibate or engaged" to that list!)

We are one in Christ, joined to Him and to one another in His death. He is the reason we get out of bed each morning, sleep fitfully through each night, and can, just maybe, even find contentment and—dare we say it?—joy! in our singleness.

Chapter 4

History Is on Your Side

The authors of Holy Scripture weren't the only ones interested in writing about marriage. Theologians and historians alike have much to say about the subjects of singleness, chastity, virginity, and spouses. Like pastors and doctors of theology today, the Church Fathers spent considerable time lauding the benefits of virginity, perhaps due in part to the rising popularity of living the celibate life in service to the Church. On the flip side, Ephesians 5 was still the very heartbeat of understanding and expounding upon what the roles and duties and attitudes of husbands and wives were to be.

This may come as a shock to you—and pretty much everyone between the ages of 14 and 95—but the Christian ideal of abstaining from sex until marriage has historically been quite commendable. (And from what my guy friends tell me, it's still intensely attractive.) "The more corrupt society becomes, the more value virtue and virginity will probably have with the kind of man a girl would wish to marry."[1] In the Church's early centuries, chastity and virginity were extolled virtually above all else, even marriage, due in large part to the single person's ability to "earnestly desire the higher gifts" (1 Corinthians 12:31), those that cause and cultivate a life of service to Christ and His Church. (It turns out that what the world is trying to sell you—that you can mess around with whomever you want whenever you want—is actually its way of turning you into its very own guinea pig, a human lab rat. We've seen how hard it is to maintain fidelity in the midst of thousands of years of preaching about the blessings of virginity, but what will our world look like when we are extolling the exact opposite for the same amount of time? Wait. Don't tell us. We don't really want to know.)

Not to worry, though! For those whom the Lord blesses with a spouse, the Church Fathers have something to say to you too. Marriage, children, the roles of husbands and wives, and the joys inherent in each of them, were all cause for pages of theological exposition at the pens of those who gave form and shape to the Early Church. For instance, Tertullian, who wrote extensively in the second and third centuries, acknowledged that for most people, even Christians, "the flesh is weak" (Matthew 26:41), making it difficult to renounce the pleasures—sexual and otherwise—of the world in comparison to living lives wholly devoted to Christ and none other. Acknowledging this, he praised those who are given and eventually marry a man or woman of firm faith. This union, he noted, causes even God the Father and all His holy angels to rejoice. "How beautiful, then, the marriage of two Christians, two who are one in hope, one in desire, one in the way of life they follow, one in the religion they practice. . . . They are, in very truth, two in one flesh."[2]

But Tertullian, perhaps more than any of the other Church Fathers who wrote on the topics of singleness and marriage, didn't stop there. Couples bound together in Christ had much work left to do.

> *They pray together, they worship together, they fast together. . . . Side by side they visit God's church and partake of God's Banquet; side by side they face difficulties and persecution, share their consolations. They have no secrets from one another; they never shun each other's company; they never bring sorrow to each other's hearts. Unembarrassed they visit the sick and assist the needy. They give alms without anxiety; they attend the Sacrifice without difficulty; they perform their daily exercise of piety without hindrance. They need not be furtive about making*

the Sign of the Cross, nor timorous in greeting the
brethren, nor silent in asking a blessing of God.
Psalms and hymns they sing to one another. . . .
Hearing and seeing this, Christ rejoices.[3]

Both a duty and a joy, the joint work of a married couple was not only for their own benefit but also set a good precedent for others. A Christian marriage does much to combat the bad examples of relationships set by the culture, the world, and the people in it. So whether someone was single, like Paul, or married, like Tertullian, Christians and their relationships were identifying marks of the Body of Christ, set apart for holy work in whatever station Christ placed them.

Chrysostom: Fair in God's Sight

Chrysostom, a humble fourth-century monk who wound up as the bishop of Constantinople, championed the single life as well. (See? You have all sorts of important pastors in your corner!) He spent much of his early years echoing the words of Paul: "To the unmarried and the widows I say that it is good for them to remain single as I am" (1 Corinthians 7:8). Virginity was to be preferred over chastity, he taught, since it is a temptation, especially for women, to get caught up in all things worldly when it came to relationships: finances, clothes, even their own looks.

Chrysostom explained his reasoning: virginity was more than simply not having sex before taking one's wedding vows, he noted. Instead, the difference between a virgin and a wife was a woman's focus and concentration, that on which she spent her time. A woman who was strong in faith and fervent in love for the Church and for her neighbor espoused all that was good about virginity. A woman who was married was deterred from "devoting all her strength to a life of prayer,"[4] but the reasons, he said, were noble and praiseworthy: respecting her husband, managing her household, and loving her children.

Chrysostom didn't leave the men out. He wrote extensively on how to find and choose a wife, encouraging men to do the hard work of sorting out wheat from the chaff before the marriage instead of after. The qualities a man ought to look for, he said, were not fleeting things, such as beauty or her ability to fill out a dress just right. (All right, those are my words. We're paraphrasing here.)

Instead, he instructed young men instead to look for things that please Christ. Among those were modesty, decency, and a tender demeanor. "Look for affection, gentleness, and humility in a wife. . . . Let us make her fair in God's sight, not in our own."[5] He told men to look for a woman with a strong confession of Christ, who is faithful and kind, who doesn't seek to lead when she ought to follow or direct her husband when he is the head of the household.

But the standards were high for the men too, who were to be responsible to their wives, even to the point of the death. Marrying a woman, Chrysostom warned them, was not to be taken lightly or flippantly. (Unlike *The Real Housewives of Orange County*, Chrysostom did not condone phrases such as "Go ahead and marry him. There's always divorce." Just to clarify.)

> *Do you want your wife to be obedient to you, as the Church is to Christ? Then be responsible for the same providential care of her, as Christ is for the Church. And even if it becomes necessary for you to give your life for her, yes, and even to endure and undergo suffering of any kind, do not refuse. Even though you undergo all this, you will never have done anything equal to what Christ has done.[6]*

He wrote to the married and to the single, to those looking for a spouse and to those who, like Paul, were given to a life of chastity. But no matter a person's station in life, Chrysostom urged Christians on to the pursuit of something even better than a patient wife or a strong husband: "So whether we presently live in virginity, in our first marriage, or in our second, let us pursue holiness, that we may be counted worthy to see Him and to attain the Kingdom of Heaven, through the grace and love for mankind of our Lord Jesus."[7] And he was right. Christ at the center—of our relationships, our friends, and our life—is exactly where He ought to be.

Ambrose: Doctor of Virginity

A peer of Chrysostom, Ambrose, the Bishop of Milan, was also firm in his belief that singles have much to teach the rest of the Church. (In fact, he wrote so much on the topics of sexual purity and chastity that he was given the title "Doctor of Virginity"!) But Ambrose also wrote extensively about something else: that marriage itself is a divine gift so perfect, in fact, that it provided a way to salvation. For Ambrose, the equation of one man plus one woman in Christ results in—by His grace—the procreation of children. Ambrose believed firmly the psalmist's words: "Behold, children are a heritage from the LORD, the fruit of the womb a reward" (Psalm 127:3), reminding Christians that children bring holy joy to a marriage. While discussions still occur among Christian churches today as to whether marriage actually qualifies as a sacrament (some, including the Roman Catholic Church, say it is; others say it is not), Ambrose ladled praise on both states, single and married, as long as the Christian remained in his or her rightful posture of looking only to Christ for fulfillment and completion.

Ambrose mimicked Paul in much of his writing, encouraging those who were unmarried to stay that way if they were able, since marriage bears with it an implicit amount of its own unique burdens and unfulfilled promises. He also wrote extensively on the concept that those who were able to remain celibate were nobler than those who were married. Before you get too bent out of shape, keep in mind that Ambrose meant this in the sense that, because a single person can and must rely on Christ alone and not on the words or affirmation or support of a spouse, he or she could be dedicated to the Christian life in a way that others could not and in a way that others probably could not even understand.

Finally, the bishop held up what he believed to be the best example of purity and virginity from the Scriptures: Mary, the mother of our Lord. Ambrose urged Christians to let her life and piety give form and shape to their own prayers and desire to remain pure and chaste with regard to sexuality. And he was on to something, because Mary's virginity provides a road map for those who continue to wait on the Lord. When her life took a dramatic turn, when nothing made sense, when the Lord asked more of her than she thought she could handle, when He placed on her suffering unique to her, Mary responded calmly and in faith, "Behold, I am the servant of the Lord; let it be to me according to your word" (Luke 1:38). Many of us have struggled to pray that the Lord's will would be done in our singleness. More often, we're the ones telling the Lord how He ought to answer our prayers. May Mary's faith and trust in the promises of her Savior be such an example of waiting on the Lord for all of us who are single!

Some scholars contend that Ambrose wrote so much on the subject of virginity that he was actually anti-marriage, and when such passages "are taken from their context, it seems that he discourages marriage."[8] Instead, it appears he "favors [virginity] above marriage, but he assures us, not to the detriment of marriage."[9] But Ambrose doesn't stop when discussing virginity. Instead, throughout his writing, he makes clear that he is not speaking unfavorably of marriage but is instead lifting up its counterpart: the ideal of virginity. (And we can't blame him. Perhaps if we as Christians today spoke as well of a chaste life as we do of married life, the world would have a harder time making a mockery of it!)

In distinguishing between those who are married and those who are yet single, Ambrose teaches us that there is an order to the "holy work" of married life, even as there is an order to the life of a single person. And the order, no matter the person, begins and ends with Christ. Because whether a person is married or single or dating or a widow(er), he or she is a part of the Church. And when a person is a part of the Church, he is a part of the Body of Christ: one, holy, and perfect. And when Ambrose puts it that way, we can't but think he just may be on to something.

Luther: Marriage as Gift and Favor

Luther, as you might have guessed, wasn't silent on the subject either. A celibate monk in his early years, he eventually married a nun and fathered his own family, thus providing a unique perspective on the two drastically different lifestyles. But if the Early Church Fathers spoke more often of virginity, Luther evened the scale when it came to the topic of marriage. He encouraged young men and women not to be ashamed of their natural desire for the opposite sex, writing, "There is nothing disgraceful about it. Celibacy is supposed to be a virtue, but it is a veritable miracle of God, just as if a person did not eat or drink. . . . There are not many virgins to whom God granted a long life; rather hurriedly He whisked them out of this world, like Cecilia, Agnes, Lucia, Agatha, and others like them. I know full well how noble that treasure is, but also how difficult it is to preserve for any length of time" (Luther's Works 52:273).

Luther's context warranted this kind of discussion. Combating the Roman Catholic Church's contention that the priesthood—and its accompanying celibacy—was a more holy vocation than any other, Luther bucked the trend.

> *Whoever finds himself unsuited to the celibate life*
> *should see to it right away that he has something to*
> *do and to work at; then let him strike out in God's*
> *name and get married. . . . Let God worry about how*
> *they and their children are to be fed. God makes*
> *children; he will surely also feed them. Should he*
> *fail to exalt you and them here on earth, then take*
> *satisfaction in the fact that he has granted you a*
> *Christian marriage, and know that he will exalt*
> *you there; and be thankful to him for his gifts and*
> *favors.* (Luther's Works 45:46–49)

(It's also worth noting that, in this same breath, Luther says that men ought to get married at age 18 and women no later than age 15. We are now at almost double that number. Women, on average, get married at age 27 and men at age 29. Let's get cracking, people!) Luther's point was this: marriage is a great blessing and a rich honor. "It is an excellent thing and a matter of divine seriousness" (Large Catechism I 208), he explained. Even Philip Melanchthon, Luther's compatriot who authored the Augsburg Confession, wrote, "God has commanded that marriage be honored" (XXXIV 19). So let it be written; so let it be done!

Pope John Paul II: Attitudes and Values

Finally, Pope John Paul II wrote extensively on the exceptionality of celibacy and the beauty of marriage, describing them as two vocations that complement each other, due in part to their "significance and manifold importance."

> *In the life of an authentically Christian community*
> *the attitudes and values proper to the one and the*
> *other state—that is, to one or the other essential*
> *and conscious choices as a vocation for one's*
> *entirely earthly life and in the perspective of the*
> *"heavenly Church"—complete and in a certain sense*
> *interpenetrate each other.*[10]

So, if you struggle with being single, if you think that being alone stinks and is generally the pits, if you don't want to be by yourself one second more, if you are tired of making all your own decisions and living with your one-eyed cat; if you are single and okay with it, if it's neither here nor there, if there are days when you love your freedom and days when you find it overrated, if the Lord has given you the gift of celibacy and you are content in your singleness, if you have been married and are divorced, or if you knew the joys of marriage but now live as one widowed, take heart. You are not the first, nor will you be the last. You are numbered among the faithful saints who have endured the burden of being unmarried and who were sustained by our Lord along the way. Why else would authors spend so much time on the subject if you didn't matter?

Because whether you have chosen your singleness or whether the Lord has given it to you, whether you are content with your current situation or whether you hate it with a deep and intense loathing, whether you long for relationships that no longer are or whether you simply remember them with a quiet joy, you feel. You feel deeply. You are, perhaps, more in tune with your feelings than most. You have time to think on and understand what you feel because you *are* alone, because you have time to reflect on what it would mean to have a companion, why you want this place in life to continue or not for you.

For a long time, my little nephew Jonathan wouldn't talk about the darkness in his room when the lights were turned out. He called it "the deepness." (Little ones are remarkably perceptive that way.)

The cross of being single is just that: sometimes dark, sometimes deep, but always wide. It never stops; it never quits. Sometimes it ebbs and flows, waning or strengthening with the seasons of the year, weddings of friends, Valentine's Day, and chocolate (and its proximity to the single person devouring it). But for most, the deepness, the longing, is never completely absent.

There is a temptation here to despair, to doubt the Lord's goodness. It becomes easy to refuse to go to church, certain that God has nothing left to give you. You forget that there is a difference between being alone and being lonely. You pray fervently for a spouse. And then you stop praying, sure that the Lord's good gift of marriage is not for you. You resign yourself to a life you didn't imagine, one you didn't want.

But then, in His perfect time and in His perfect way, the Lord answers your prayers, the prayers of the faithful on your behalf, the groanings and intercedings of the Holy Spirit when tears and anger and apathy kept you from calling upon your heavenly Father. In answering that prayer, He gives you the perfect gift, the one perfectly matched to you, the one that fills all the holes your suffering creates. You may not realize it. It may not feel like it. Perhaps it's not the answer you wanted, or perhaps it is. Maybe it's the gift of contentment. Maybe it's the gift of a spouse. Maybe it's the gift of simply surviving. Maybe it's the gift of pure joy or the ability to endure the cross He's given you with a grace that bears witness to Christ to others. Because despite our propensity to give up and give in, despite our disbelief that the Lord really does know what He's doing, His plan is always good and perfect and best. Despite the evidence. Despite proof of the opposite. Despite your feelings.

The world isn't ending. Being single isn't the worst fate to befall mankind. You will survive. You will find joy. Life won't always be grim. The Lord sees and answers, drawing the broken-hearted to Him with a tender love that alone can alleviate all suffering, all grief, all pain.

There is better news still! He provides this comfort in tangible, earthly ways. He doesn't just tell you that you are loved. He gives you those

> His plan is always good and perfect and best.

things that you can lay hold of, touch, feel, taste, and hear to know that you are indeed loved and that you are not alone. Each Sunday, He puts a man, a pastor, in your midst to tell you—yes, you personally—that you are a child loved by God; to pronounce His forgiveness on you for all the times you've doubted the Lord and His will for your life; to remind you that the Lord will not allow more hardship to enter your life than you can handle.

This same man the Lord puts behind your church's Communion rail, locating him in a position where he can put onto your tongue and into your mouth the very body and blood of the Man who knows and understands separation and loneliness more acutely than any other, even than you. This man gives you Jesus in a concrete way for your benefit, for you, so that you have no reason to doubt whether forgiveness and comfort and love and joy are yours in Christ.

This pastor is the one the Lord has put in a chair in an office, seated across from an open chair that has your name on it. He is there to listen to your fears, to share in your heartbreak, to celebrate your joys with you, and to tell you again and again that nothing is able to separate you from your Father. He is there to care for you, to bear the burden with you. He is there to be, yes, he *wants* to be your pastor.

We are all little doubting Thomases. Alone with our thoughts, we find it easy to forget that we matter to Christ, to lag in our prayers, to slide into disbelief. But Christ puts our pastors, our churches, our Christian friends and family in our way, little speed bumps to slow us down, to remind us that this is not the end, to give us hope, to walk with us out of the deepness.

And we do.

My Soul Waits for the Lord

Well, it happened again. I just received a call from yet another friend who shared with me the wonderful news that she is expecting. My first thought is overwhelming joy for this dear friend and the blessings that await her. It's the second thought that concerns me, haunts me. Filled with tremendous sorrow for the ever-growing vacancy in my heart, I plea to God, "Why, Lord? I feel I have been patient. Will You ever answer the cry of my heart?"

We are taught from an early age that Christ's unconditional love is sufficient for us all. Yet we [women] have this desire in our hearts to model the Proverbs 31 wife and to follow God's command to be fruitful and multiply.

Every Sunday in worship, we are reminded of our singleness. We walk through the doors of the church, where families are gathering their children for worship. We sit in the pew alone. We eagerly seek the words of wisdom flowing from the Scriptures, sharing the message of Christ's love for us. Just look how many times the word *love* is mentioned in the Bible! And then it happens. In the excitement and vigor of his sermon, Pastor cries out from the pulpit praise for the blessings of families and children, and my heart breaks a little more. Where do I fit in this picture? Never has he mentioned the treasure singles can bring to the church: the value and heart for service, the longing for connection and the love and fellowship shared by those in the Body of Christ.

It's not the churches' fault they have failed to understand this aching desire. After all, Scripture tells us what a wonderful blessing we find in marriage and children. However, what do we do in the meantime? How can the church help us find joy in our singleness? There are a multitude of opportunities for service to God. Recognize and utilize the gifts and talents of your single members to further the Gospel of Christ. Seek them out as a benefit rather than a blight on your congregation.

I have been praying for my future husband since 2000—too many long years of receiving phone call after phone call announcing engagements, weddings, and babies. I haven't experienced the excitement and anticipation of a bride for her bridegroom or felt the first kick of a baby in my womb, and I may never have those experiences. But I take comfort in the knowledge of Christ's love for me. Every day I wake in the knowledge of Christ and say another prayer that He will fulfill the desires of my heart in His time, not mine.

And as I sit here, my soul waits for the Lord.

—Christine, mid-thirties

Chapter 5

Lonely, Lame, and Overrated:
The Road Well Traveled

They were packed into the room, college students from all over the United States. Sitting on the floor, leaning against the wall, sharing a seat: it didn't matter. They were attending a conference on what it means to be a faithful, bold Lutheran, but today, they only wanted to hear what I had to share with them about what it means to live as a single person in this world.

"You all are here for the sectional on speed dating, right?" I asked nonchalantly, looking up from my papers on the podium. Their faces froze. One girl's eyes dashed nervously to the door, and she looked for a second like she might actually make a break for it.

Then I winked. "Kidding!"

They all laughed. And by "laughed" I mean "let out one big, slightly panicked sigh of relief."

"My friend suggested that I title this presentation 'Dressing like a Hooker and Acting like a Feminist Will Not Get You the Husband You Secretly Want, and a Thousand Other Reasons Embracing Traditional Values Will Make You Happier and More Content,' but that's kind of awkward for you men, so . . ." I continued.

They laughed again. Shoulders relaxed. Faces smiled. In moments, they had gone from tense to relieved. But I had already spotted it: the angst and worry that even the thought of dating had caused.

"Let's start with definitions. I say 'single.' You say . . ." I asked the group.

"Lonely," said one girl.

"Lame," said a young man leaning against a wall in the back.

"Overrated," his buddy said.

"It's okay," shrugged one young woman, seemingly indifferent. Then, from one girl in the front, a defiant, "Freedom!"

It was quiet for a minute as all the young students turned to look her way (maybe because she yelled the word with all the gusto of a Civil War–era commander of the cavalry, ready to lead a rowdy crowd of mounted militia into battle, but that's neither here nor there). No one seemed to believe her, even as she answered my follow-up questions: Why is freedom important to you? Would you ever give up your freedom for another person?

From our minute-long interaction, it became clear to us all: the culture has had its way with our youth, our middle-aged, our elderly, Christian and non-Christian alike. The culture has taught us that freedom is to be prized above all else, that women are just like men, that a man doesn't need a woman and she doesn't need him either, that the solitary life is the preferable one.

Here's the kicker: it's all one big joke. (Side note: Now, there's something to be said here for those to whom the Lord has given the gift of celibacy. And that, by the way, doesn't seem to be a lot of us.)

Back to freedom. If we have anything to thank the 1960s and '70s for (and we do: Post-It notes, Pop Rocks, liposuction, Egg McMuffins—I can keep this up all day, people—laser printers, artificial hearts, *cell phones*), it's certainly not that which severely messed up our understanding of femininity. (If you're a guy, you should definitely, definitely stop reading here, unless you want to know why the women you're trying to date may or may not have some issues. Then keep reading. Definitely, definitely keep reading.)

Enter the sixties and seventies, followed closely by their boisterous little sister: feminism! (Now, before you Baby Boomers start chanting, "Equality now!" I'm talking here strictly of the way in which the movement changed the roles between men and women. You can quibble over the politics with your grandpa later. Chill.)

Then	Now
Women said, "Why, thank you!" when men opened doors for them.	Women snarl, "I can do it myself!" when men open doors for them.
Women believed that the vocations of wife and mother were noble.	At President Obama's installation, newspaper headlines bemoaned the fact that Michelle Obama was "stepping down" from being a Harvard Law grad to "First Wife and Mom."
Women expected men to pay for their dinner while out on a date.	If men even offer to pay for a date, they proceed to do an awkward dance with their dates, wallets half out of purses and pockets, credit cards being yanked out and then shoved back in, while the man and woman glance sideways at the check, unsure of who should pay for what. The confused waitress finally says, "Um, should I, like, get two tickets?" while the couple collapses in relief.
Women, while still having pre-marital sex, exhibited a sense of shame.	*Jersey Shore.*

The world wasn't perfect before the sixties and seventies. Women behaved in ways unbecoming to their femininity. They slept with men outside of the confines of the marriage bed. They had children out of wedlock. They subverted the order put in place in the Garden of Eden. (For those of you late to the party, it goes like this: "Then the man said, 'This at last is bone of my bones and flesh of my flesh; she shall be called Woman, because she was taken out of Man.' Therefore a man shall leave his father and his mother and hold fast to his wife, and they shall become one flesh" [Genesis 2:23-24].) They cheated on their husbands. They spoke unkindly to men, making them feel weak and disrespected. They scorned the love of good men. They were obnoxious. But they also felt and exhibited public and private shame, at least to a certain degree.

The women of the sixties and seventies slept around too. They had children outside of wedlock. They messed up the order of creation. (For those of you late to the—oh; we've been down that road

already, haven't we?) They cheated on their husbands and disrespected the men in their lives. They were obnoxious. But they were
all right with it, even proud of it. They championed it and smeared
it in the faces of men. This was the new empowered woman, the
one who didn't need a man to get what she wanted in life. And she
certainly didn't need him to feel loved and cherished.

Resetting the Moral-o-Meter

"There was another problem with the secular feminist think-
ers we studied," explains Colleen Carol Campbell. "For all of their
criticism of men's fixation on money, sex, power, and status, most
of these women obsessed over the very same things. They harped
on which perks and privileges men had that women did not. I could
see the logic behind some of their complaints, but their materialistic
worldview felt stifling. There was no transcendent horizon, few references to truth, beauty, goodness, or God. It was all about what you
could see, taste, and touch. I found nothing that spoke to the thirst
inside me that material pleasures had failed to slake."[1]

She wasn't alone. Those years were formative and, during them,
feminism changed the moral-o-meter of America. It made what was
wrong right. It made what was right old-fashioned and uncool. It
made what was kept in private public. It turned morals and values
into jokes and gags. It chipped away at what had, for so long, been a
virtuous code that, at least in a general sense, worked.

America's not been the same since. We're not any worse sinners
now that we were a few decades ago, but we have lost our ability to
be ashamed over our actions. Suddenly, we've got issues, and we're
proud of them. We're all out of whack, and we're okay with it. We're
a wreck, and that's just how we want it to be. Mothers of high school
daughters teach them to have safe sex instead of no sex. Fathers
tell their college-age sons to be careful instead of respectful when
it comes to women. Women have children who have no fathers in
the home. Fathers abandon their children, leaving the church or
state or grandparents to care for them instead. An understanding of
masculinity and femininity has been lost, and no one seems all that
interested in recovering it.

This is the norm, we are led to believe. This is how life is, we're
told: filled with teenagers who indulge in acts given by God only to
those who are married; women hurting to be loved; and coldhearted

men who refuse to love even their own offspring. We see the world through sin-colored glasses, like a windshield covered in bug guts, impairing our ability to see where we're headed and unable to know when something or someone dangerous darts into our path.

Through the bug guts and broken hearts of life, the Gospel wipes the windshield clean. Christ doesn't deal in bug smears, and He doesn't leave our lives perpetually turned on their ends. The culture's norms are for those of us who are in Christ. Not Christian men. Not Christian women. We are not okay with the way in which feminism devalues women. We're not okay with the way in which it demoralizes and disrespects men. And we're not okay with the barriers it builds in the relationships between the two.

One of the worst and most dangerous ideologies promoted by feminism is a false sense of security, in thinking that men do not need women and women do not need men. In a recent *Wall Street Journal* article, a divorced French woman spoke eloquently and even excitedly about the fact that she is finally—blissfully—alone, with her cat. That's what we've come to, dear singles: actually embracing the idea of the much-feared cat lady we all warn our friends not to let us become. That's the culture speaking. That's our pride speaking. Maybe it's even the yogurt that's been in your fridge too long speaking.

> One of the worst and most dangerous ideologies promoted by feminism is a false sense of security.

To want to be unattached from another person, though, is not the way in which God intended for us to live. Outside of those who are called to celibacy, this unattachment often feels like a façade. Singles put on a brave front, but at our core, we feel like we're pretending. "We love being the fifth wheel when our friends invite us to a ball game!" we say with bright smiles. "No, really. We actually *want* to sit at the kids' table," we tell our mothers at Thanksgiving. "Valentine's Day doesn't bother me!" we laugh through gritted teeth.

But we do a lousy job at lying to others—and to ourselves too. We know what our Lord said: "It is not good that the man should be alone; I will make him a helper fit for him" (Genesis 2:18). Yet, not only does the devil, the world, and our sinful nature encourage us to be alone but they actually convince us that we're the crazy ones if we believe anything else! "The idea of marriage has been so badly eroded, damaged, and weakened by pathologies," Dr. Robert George once explained to a group of us sitting in a lecture. "It begins with [Margaret] Sanger. And then it's the teens and twenties, and then [Alfred] Kinsey's phony, fraudulent science in the forties, and [Hugh] Hefner's soft porn, and then, if you believe in traditional marriage, you have hang-ups and you're twisted up and aren't letting people be free."

That's why the culture says, "I don't need anybody," and why our Lord say right back, "Oh, yes, you do." The culture says, "I can be with a different person every night, and it doesn't matter," and our Lord says, "I make a helper unique to the person." The culture says, "I don't need to be attached," and our Lord says, "I've got just the person for you, and I'll teach you both why it's best if you stay together for life!"

Feminism tells women that they are free, that they don't need men, that they can do it all by themselves. The culture tells men that it can use women for fun without regard for their well-being. But Jesus is here to say, "You are free in Me. If it is My will, I will find you a helper suitable for you. And you can relax. Rely on Me. I've got this."

And He does.

$$**$$

CHILL OUT. YOU'RE NOT STARTING A REVOLUTION.

Our culture's trek from a pro-marriage culture to an "It's revolutionary and hip to choose to be single; now watch me Instagram the heart-shaped cream in my coffee while I tell you again why I hate men" society has harmed the way in which men and women interact. It's set up false realities and expectations. Men expect women not to be hurt when they use them for casual sex or don't return their calls or tell them half-truths to get them to join them for a drink. Women expect men to know that, even though they say they don't care if he ever calls, they really do want him to call them back, even after a one-night stand. Our young people expect that this is the norm, because the world and society tells them that it is. The bigger problem? Their parents and friends aren't disputing it.

Watch an episode of *I'm Having Their Baby*, and you'll see, almost across the board, a steady drumbeat of single women with two or three children from different fathers—fathers who not only have no intention of marrying their children's mother, but who also choose not to support the children financially or emotionally. "Marriage and relationships are messed up enough already," the world says. "This is just proof that it's easier and safer to go through life alone!"

That's a hard one to disagree with, especially when we see divorce all around us, failed relationships in our own families, and the push for same-sex marriage on the rise in the media and the Capitol. But instead of throwing our hands up in the air and bemoaning our fate, we as the church have a chance to make a bold and faithful witness to what a Christ-centered relationship can and should look like. We can be purposeful in promoting and uplifting healthy, stable friendships where singles and married alike are valued. Here's one idea to get us started: Hey, world, stop promoting hookups, sexting, and, in general, sexual morasses.

Bam. Problem solved. World hunger, you're up next.

All right, not so fast.

What may seem like an unconquerable challenge isn't. We have God's Word—unchanging and unbeatable—on our lips and in our hearts, which puts us in the unique position of not always fretting about our current situation, but of finding ways to speak about the joys and benefits of Christ-centered dating, marriage, and life in general. Here are a few ideas to start our own counter-cultural revolution when it comes to dating, marriage, men, women, and even sex.

MEN—DO AND DON'T

DO Treat women as human beings. This means doing a lot of listening. It also will require that you pay attention to what they say and try your best to hear them. Focus when they talk. Pray that the Lord would help you view women not as sexual objects to be lusted after, but as baptized children loved by God. Remind them that they have value on account of Christ. Show them the same respect you would want shown to your mother, or your sisters, maybe even your grandma, or—gasp—one day, your daughter.

DON'T Treat women like, well, they're a chore. Because they're not. They're a gift to you, meant to fill in where you lack and be in your corner no matter what. Once you begin to look at each woman in your life as a person for whom Christ died, your understanding of her importance and value will change dramatically. Can you imagine? Your high school friend, the gal who shares a cubicle wall, your pastor's wife—these are the women for whom He gave His life. Because of Him, you can give them your respect.

DO Hold out for marriage. Part of what it means to be a husband is to take on the burden and task of protecting your wife. You'll protect her, care for her, even take a bullet for her. As for her, she's putting her life in your hands, risking it all, counting on you to care for her. That's no small thing. You can start to mirror that relationship already by acting in a way that befits a woman for whom you would risk your life, and that means keeping close tabs on your virginity and sexuality until she's your wife.

DON'T Sleep with a different person every night. No, seriously. Don't. Here's why: (1) All of the women you're tempted to sleep with are not your wives. (2) In fact, you're very likely sleeping with someone else's future wife. You're creating a relationship with a woman that's meant for her husband alone. (3) It chips away at your ability to have true, meaningful relationships. I'm not saying it's not possible, but it does affect your behavior, your ability to love, and how you see women. (4) It makes you coarse, hardened to others and to the world. (5) Our Lord tells you not to. So there.

DO Cultivate healthy female relationships outside of the dating world. Not so close to your mom? Work at being a better son. Can't stand your grandma? Pray for patience in obeying the Fourth Commandment. It's important to start this now, before you're even married. It gives you a chance to sort through some of your own frustrations and issues, and that's hard work, which your wife will appreciate and for which she will love you.

DON'T Be disrespectful. These are the women who raised you, who love you, who have prayed for your health and success even when you haven't wanted it. They are deserving of your kindness, your respect, and your time. Real men respect women, seeing them through the lens of the cross. If the Creator of the world—and of you!—prizes and cherishes them enough to die for them, you can at least stand not to be a lippy jerk.

DO Look women in the eye when they're talking. And even when they're not.

DON'T Stare at—well—just keep your eyes on their face. Trust me on this one. And that elevator thing you do with your eyes, where you start at our faces, look to our legs, and then move back up to our faces again—that's just creepy.

MEN—DO AND DON'T

DO Say no to pornography. "Sadly, 28 percent of 'born again' Christians also believe that there is nothing wrong with viewing porn, Matthew 5:28 not withstanding ('But I tell you that anyone who looks at a woman lustfully has already committed adultery with her in his heart'). But even sadder is the finding by *World* magazine that nearly 50 percent of Christians and 37 percent of their pastors admit to having a problem with pornography themselves."[2] We'll talk more on this later, but pray for God to be merciful, giving you the strength to resist the temptation to look at graphic content that hurts your faith, harms your brain, and injures your relationships.

DON'T Look at pornography. "Pornography is a drug that produces an addictive neurochemical trap, 'past reason hunted, and no sooner had, past reason hated,' as Shakespeare put it in Sonnet 129. . . . It is a cruel master, and seeks more slaves."[3] It's easy to write off porn, claiming that it's not a drug and therefore can't be an addiction. But it can and it is. It affects the way the frontal lobe of your brain works, your ability to feel joy and excitement with your wife when you do marry, and your capacity to live physically and emotionally stable lives. Stay away. "Pornography wants you, it wants your husband or wife, it wants your son and daughter, your grandchildren, and your in-laws. It doesn't share well, and it doesn't leave easily."[4]

———————————————————————

DO Listen. A woman adores a man who is willing to listen to her, even if you're never going to end up dating her. It bespeaks a maturity, a genuineness, a real manliness that she craves.

DON'T Tune out. Women talk a lot. We know. We like to emote. Sometimes—all right, most times—we take ten minutes to tell you a story that should have taken us five. But do us a favor: Shut off the game. Put down the hot wings. Set the beer on the coaster. Give us just a few minutes of your time. You'll understand us better, we'll think you're awesome, and all of us will come out ahead. And next time, when you've had an awful day and need to do some talking of your own, we'll be more than eager to listen.

———————————————————————

DO Be assertive. Be bold. Be brave. If you need help or want advice, ask for it. That's what you men do; you problem solve. There's no shame in asking your friends or family or pastor for ideas or thoughts when it comes to being single or dating.

DON'T Wimp out. Letting someone else make the decisions while you lay on the couch isn't really all that appealing. While we're at it, if you're going to ask a girl out, man, ask her out. Don't "Well, I'll do whatever you want to do." Don't "I don't really know any good restaurants, so if you have any ideas, we can just do whatever." Have a plan. State it. And then wait for her answer. Because, seriously, the "wah, wah, waaaaaaaah" of that sad trombone playing in the background isn't working for us either.

———————————————————————

DO Delve into the Word. Read it. Ponder it. Pray it. Talk about it. God's Word works, even when you aren't aware of it. You want to be a strong man of God? Go to the source.

DON'T Skip church. Jesus was a man, and He has a lot to teach you about your masculinity. Go to the place where He can help you grow in that manliness.

———————————————————————

WOMEN—DO AND DON'T

DO Dress modestly. There are certain kinds of clothes that make us feel better about ourselves, that give us a waist, that show off our curves, that make us feel feminine and confident. But despite how amazing your mom says you are, sweetie, it's actually not all about you. There's these other people in the world (they're called men), and often times, the clothes we wear don't exactly help them focus. That's not helpful. In fact, it's so not helpful, it's hurtful. So, watch what you wear. You're not Amish, but you are a woman of God. Respect His beautiful design in you, and find some longer shorts and higher-cut tops. For all our sakes.

DON'T Wear a skirt so short that it reveals your gender when you sit down. Sweetheart, there's some parts of your body only your husband and your doctor should see, and those are it. Instead, let's work on our wardrobes and choose to wear things, especially to church, more suited to being in the presence of the God of creation who comes to meet us there. We can also choose to think more of our neighbor, of our pastors, of the guys we interact with than we do of ourselves, and then dress in a way that bears witness to the snazzy, classy creations God made us to be. Really, did you ever see Audrey Hepburn in shorts so short her pockets were sticking out? Child, please.

DO Be judicious. Just because a guy asks you out doesn't mean you have to go. But just because a guy doesn't seem like your type doesn't mean that you shouldn't. (See what I did there?)

DON'T Say no to every guy who invites you on a date. If he's not a serial killer, seems semi-pleasant, and won't hurt you, go for coffee. It's all right. If he is a serial killer, a jerk, and has a bad attitude, cut him loose and go hang with your girls.

DO Protect your virginity. Our Lord has given you a commandment in this very regard, one that bids you to "Fear and love God so that we lead a sexually pure and decent life in what we say and do" (Luther's Small Catechism, Sixth Commandment). It's for your protection; your spiritual, mental, and physical care; and for the safety of all your future relationships, including your potential husband. Just because a guy tells you you're beautiful doesn't mean you give him that which you can only give up once. That gift is for your husband alone.

DON'T Sleep with every guy who tells you you're beautiful. If you're going to follow that route, you're going to be a very, very busy woman indeed. There are good men in the world—thoughtful Christian men—who want to care for you in the ways that they ought. But there are also a lot of men who can't think beyond their plumbing. They know what to say, what you want to hear, and how often they need to pay attention to both to get one of a woman's most prized possessions—the gift of sexuality—from you. Hold out. Stand firm. Pray for patience. Resolve to care enough about yourself not to be degraded as someone's fling. The only man who deserves to know you in that way is the one who's already told you "I do."

DO Encourage the men in your life. They need it! They need to be told that you respect them, that you value their opinion, that what they think matters to you. The more you show them respect, the more your view of them as blundering idiots will begin to morph and change. Pray for them, comfort them, support them, and care for them. Remind them of what it means to be a man—gently and kindly— when they are tempted to give up, be lazy, worry, and not fulfill their duties. And if, by God's grace, one day you are no longer single and are given the gift of children, raise strong, Christian sons,

WOMEN—DO AND DON'T

teaching them from their youth about who Christ is, what He has done, and how His death on the cross transforms lives for eternity.

DON'T Disregard your dads and brothers. Bad idea! You may not have a husband or boyfriend yet, but you can begin to model healthy, adult relationships even with those in your circle of friends or in your family. Do you interrupt your grandpa? Do you give your brother two choices for dinner, and then go with the opposite of what he said? Do you roll your eyes when your dad is sharing something with you? Stop doing that. It's (1) annoying and (2) unbecoming a lady. Listen, show respect, and calm down. You may be a woman, but nobody wants to hear you roar.

DO Find faithful Christian female mentors. The most natural person is your mother, but if she's not the greatest role model or is no longer living, or if your relationship is strained, seek out women at church. They have much to teach, and you have much to learn.

DON'T Assume you are way smarter than everyone else, because that almost never works out well for everybody involved. Instead, spend time with women who rejoice in the goodness and faithfulness of the Lord and are humble, faithful, maternal, and joyful. Learn from women who have struggled through life's sorrows and have still proclaimed, "The Lord gave, and the Lord has taken away; blessed be the name of the Lord" (Job 1:21). Sit at the feet of those who model repentance and piety, show eager and real sorrow over their sins, and desire true forgiveness where they have erred. That, in turn, will bring about for you a life lived in forgiveness, joy, and understanding.

DO Look at a man's heart. I dated a line of men because they were in the military. (Let's all do ourselves a favor and just acknowledge that I'm only here to serve as a horrible example for you of what not to do. I'll send you the bill later.) I liked the idea of men who were tough, disciplined, and assertive, and I assumed that I could find that type of guy in an organization that calls for being all of those things. (It also didn't hurt that they all looked good in uniforms.) But a handsome face and a six-pack do not a relationship make. Don't let your eyes deceive you; hold out for a man who is just that—a man—one who cares more for you than about himself, who puts your needs above his own, who asks how your day went before launching into his own problems, who makes you his priority. Because if he has all of those qualities, you will want to care for and love him right back, and I kind of think that's how the Lord designed it to work.

DON'T Date a dude for his credit card, hair, or motorcycle. You can do that, but I almost guarantee you'll have your heart broken, and broken hearts really stink. Trends are fleeting; money is easily lost. Relationships built on the superficial—on things that aren't guaranteed and are easily replaceable—can't and don't last. Wait for a man who loves you regardless of your checking account, who is drawn in by your heart and brain, your wit and character. Those things rarely change and infrequently fade. The man who loves you for what makes you you, not for what you purchase to accent that, is the one you want to hang on to for life.

DO Pray for a man. A real man, that is. For a long time, I wanted to marry a man who was dangerous. I wanted adventure, and guys with tattoos and motorcycles seemed to fit that bill. Then I met my husband, and I realized that I actually didn't want dangerous, that, in fact, dangerous is actually pretty

WOMEN—DO AND DON'T

lame. Pray that the Lord will give you a husband who will be the spiritual head of your family, who will fix the garbage disposal when you break it, who will warm up your side of the bed before you get into it, who will tell you he loves you when you are most frustrated with each other. Those men exist. I know. I married one.

DON'T Settle. You could get married tomorrow if you wanted to. You could. I'm serious. There are people who will marry anybody just to be married. But you have a gracious Lord, one who desires to give what's best to His children, to His daughters. So pray for Him to give you one of His children, His sons, who love Him, who desire to receive all that He has to give them, who see women as God's creation. He still makes them. I promise.

DO Evaluate your relationships. If you are in a relationship and you are working harder at it that your boyfriend is, slow down long enough to evaluate whether this man is right for you. I found myself, at one point in my first engagement, convincing my fiancé that we should be together. If you have to do that, girl, you have real, serious problems.

DON'T Let a dude use you as a doormat as long as he doesn't leave you. Women are emotional creatures. We long to be loved and hugged and told we're pretty, and we'll do almost anything to get a guy to tell us that. The danger here is that we'll let a man do anything to us in return simply to keep him around and, if we're lucky, get him to tell us we clean up nice every now and then. If the man you're with doesn't see you as a great source of joy in his life, if the amount of effort he puts into making time for you is tantamount to the amount of effort a construction worker puts in leaning on a shovel, if he ditches you to hang with his friends, if he only talks to you or calls you when it's convenient

for him, reevaluate. You are worth more than that. You're worth everything, really. Know how I know? Jesus had His palms and feet nailed to a tree for you. He gasped for breath and cried out in longing for His Father for you. And He was raised again, for you, so that you would know that you are loved, cared for, and more important than anything else in the world to Him.

DO Look at Pinterest, not at pornography. The guys just got schooled in this, but the dirty little secret is that women aren't so innocent themselves when it comes to sneaking peeks at porn. "Women account for as much as one-third of all pornographic consumption."[5] Instead, return to what Scripture commends to you, that which "is true, whatever is honorable, whatever is just, whatever is pure, whatever is lovely, whatever is commendable, if there is any excellence, if there is anything worthy of praise, think about these things" (Philippians 4:8). Ask our Lord to set your uniquely feminine heart and mind on these things, lovely and commendable things, things befitting a baptized, forgiven woman and the design with which God created her.

DON'T Sneak peeks at sketchy things online, thinking, after all, who's going to find out? Well, there's your heavenly Father, for starters. Your sins are not secret, no matter how stealthy you think you are. If you've already looked at and watched images and videos you shouldn't, repent. Talk to your pastor. Ask him to pronounce Christ's forgiveness on you. Put barriers in place on your computer to stop you from looking. Seek out a trusted friend whom you will be willing to call and who will be a listening ear when you begin to feel you are tempted beyond what you are able. A man's body is something in which his wife can find delight and pleasure, but make that joy complete. Save it for marriage.

71

WOMEN—DO AND DON'T

DO Take care of others. There is a great temptation in singleness to focus on ourselves and to get so caught up in our own suffering that we hardly recognize the pains of others. There's also no better way to stop feeling sorry for yourself than to help someone else in need. It refocuses you, reminds you that your Lord has blessed you a great deal, and turns your interests to how you can better show mercy and love to your neighbor—and that is a good thing!

DON'T Stare at your belly button. Satan would have us spend our days navel-gazing, turned in on ourselves and away from coming alongside our friends and family who need and deserve our care. Be deliberate in asking questions of your loved ones who are hurting. Ask them what they're feeling or how you can specifically pray for them. Just as you, as a single person, aren't always interested in hearing everyone else's advice, consider that this person may simply need you—at this time and in this place—to nod, to hug him or her, and simply to understand.

See how easy that was? If you want to be different, if you want to stand apart from the crowd by being a true rebel, combat the culture. Snub your nose at the dismal way in which the sixties and seventies messed up relationships that were already damaged by sin. Reject the idea that selfishness is a good reason for singleness. Discuss with your friends the harm these cultural changes have done. Pray that the Lord would keep you from desiring the focus to be on you, rather than on the person He potentially has waiting in the wings for you.

Men, step up. Be men. Lead. And women, encourage and care for them.

And now we're back to world hunger. Again.

Chapter 6

The Caste System

We interrupt this message to you singles to have a chat with those of you who are married or are pastors to singles or anyone who ever comes into contact with someone who is struggling with being single. (That basically means all of you.)

The singles in your church or community or circle of friends need your help. They are lonely, frustrated, and maybe even scared. The good news? The Lord, in His infinite wisdom, has chosen to place the two of you into each other's lives, which means that you get the joy of caring for your neighbor, showing Christ's mercy to one who is suffering. Blessed are you!

The better news? This task and blessing is pretty easy.

Step 1: Spot the singles in your church or community. It won't be hard to do. It's the easiest game of Where's Waldo? out there, minus an occasional white and red striped shirt. Just look for the ones who are sitting alone, who look tentatively around after church for someone to talk to, who are either desperate to attend every church function—eager to experience community—or who never show up, too afraid they won't have anyone to talk to or sit with.

Step 2: Validate their fears and worries, even the pain that they do their best to hide. That's all. Just assure them you know it's real, that it hurts, and that you're sorry they're suffering.

Step 3: Do your best to do away with the singles caste system, because there is one. Young singles are at the top of the list, the most socially acceptable and "normal." The widowed are next. On the bottom rung are the divorced. And if there are any given the gift of celibacy, they reside in the north forty, an area where they are left all to themselves, usually quickly labeled "unusual" or even presumed to struggle with same-sex attraction.

It's probably easy for you to sympathize with the *twenty-some-things*. Because they're still young, you can empathize and even support them. They still have their vibrancy, and youth is on their side. You expect that the Lord has good things in store for them, so it's easy to write them off since it seems they are merely experiencing a time of waiting.

The *widowed*, you no doubt think, are deserving of your pity, even if it's not your sympathy that they want. Scripture tells us to care for the orphan and the widow ("Religion that is pure and undefiled before God, the Father, is this: to visit orphans and widows in their affliction" [James 1:27]), and the biblical bidding when it comes to those whose love has been lost through no fault of their own feels easy to follow. However, it can be harder to understand their singleness if you have never experienced it yourself. Others are able to con themselves into believing that the widows have it slightly better than our young singles, since they have, at least, known love at least once in their life, which is more than we can say from some.

The *divorced* have it the worst. As sinners, those of us in the church are quick to assume that it is their fault, that if they had tried harder or been a better spouse or not argued as much, they would still be happily married. Scripture is clear on the prohibition not to divorce unless under extreme circumstances, and so we lump them into a category all their own: loved but not spoken of, cared for but not discussed.

And then there is the *celibate*, who appears to waffle in the gray of the unknown. We think at first that these men and women are simply pious Christians who have not been given to marriage, but as time wears on and years pass by, we start to mutter to one another. "He never has any dates." "She doesn't seem to be in any hurry to get married." "He spends a lot of time with that other guy; do you think they're more than friends?"

The truth is that there are many singles among us whose stories are not what we would expect, both for better and for worse. As we learn some of them now, may we also discover better ways in which to love them compassionately and kindly and, more than that, simply to listen.

Step 4: Listen and learn. You're about to read some stories from single Christians who are a variety of ages and who have experienced heartbreak in innumerable ways. Listen to the advice they have to give you. It's all yours, and it's spot-on.

TWENTY-SOMETHINGS

Our church's young people, and even those in our communities who may not be Christian, are deserving of our love. This stage of life is a particularly difficult time of testing. Sexual urges are hard to control. Emotions run deep. The need for popularity and acceptance are overwhelming. Friends are not so much encouraging them to hook up on a whim as they are explaining that doing so can't possibly hurt anything. It's not a case of "You should!" but of "What can it hurt?"

In our sex-driven society, it's not just young men and women who text one another racy pictures and end up spending the night after parties replete with red Solo cups, pot, and unmentionable activities in dirty bathrooms. It's young women with young women just as it is young men with young men. No longer do we live in a LGBT (lesbian, gay, bisexual, transgender) culture. Now we live in an LGBTQQ+ (lesbian, gay, bisexual, transgender, queer, questioning, affirming) culture. Anything goes. Literally. From Craigslist listings for every kind of deviant sexual behavior possible to prominent American universities teaching classes on bestiality, the hearts and private parts of our youth are in bold, obvious danger.

During these formative years, young people need our attention and care in deep and deliberate ways. That's where you married couples and older adults come into play. You have kitchen tables, right? Invite these young singles into your homes, even if they say no the first three times because they're too shy. You have frozen pizzas, right? Make one, and deliver it to them some night. They will be shocked and touched. You have a debit card to buy movie tickets, right? Buy an extra one. Turns out young adults like a little entertainment too. Show your care for them tangibly, even if they're not willing to open up and talk to you just yet.

Pastors, you're not off the hook either. Text the young people in your congregation every now and then to check in. Facebook them to ask how things are going and to remind them that they are in your prayers. Meet them where they are, starting communication in a format and a venue that they're comfortable with.

Every now and then, in your messages, be purposeful in reminding them that you are praying for them and for their future spouses, that the Lord would bring them together in His just-right timing. That is to say, keep God's design for their well-being at the forefront of their minds. Doing that will go a long way in making it easier for them to come to you with questions or straight-up worries when they need to.

Find ways to get them involved in the life of your congregation as well. That doesn't mean that you have to start a group just for singles. Walking into that environment can leave a guy or gal feeling like a rack of ribs at a dog shelter. Instead, create an atmosphere that will allow singles to be around and get to know healthy, well-rounded couples, families, grandparents, and professionals. Match them up with a widow who hates sitting alone in church on Sunday. Let them learn from the young couple who just got married and are finding their way through the first year of married life. Make purposeful mention of singles in your sermons and Bible studies. Connect them up with the empty-nesters who absolutely adored raising their children and would love to find a person for whom they can pray and with whom they can spend a Sunday brunch. Get them time with a grandma or grandpa in your congregation, with someone who can offer sage, wise advice about marriage, children, and what matters in this life. Teach them without teaching them; simply provide them with opportunities to learn from faithful, sound Christians who have made progress in this regard.

Beyond that, ask them for their help. Young singles want to be able to contribute to the life of the church and to their communities. They may not be able to make the midday Bible study due to work or class, but they can edit church newsletters (we're pretty awesome at tech stuff, in case you didn't know), help plan church game nights, or organize an outing for the youth group. Put them to work, and let them discover—on their own—that the church needs them, that they're a vital part of the Body of Christ, that we all care for one another, regardless of our age or gender or marital status.

For those of you who have single children or who know singles in your congregation or who come into any kind of contact with those whom our Lord hasn't yet blessed with a spouse, recognize, too, that our young ones especially are desperate for love, and they will get it however they can find it. Women, especially, fall prey to, as the saying goes, "looking for love in all the wrong places." If their relationships with their fathers were sketchy, if Dad wasn't around much or didn't articulate his love, if—God forbid—he abused them, then desiring and finding a healthy relationship can be one of the most trying experiences a woman may go through.

This is when you as the church can and must step up to the plate in love. That, after all, is what we do. In this way, "God settles the solitary in a home" (Psalm 68:6). He places the singles into families. And you, the church, are the family.

So do it. Mothers, smother the young singles. Ask them if they're eating their vegetables and getting enough sleep and getting to work on time. Fathers, direct these young men and women. If they're doing something stupid, call them out on it, and then come alongside to encourage and support them. Be their parents in that place, judiciously and graciously.

> You as the church can and must step up to the plate in love.

Listen. Put on your mom and dad ears, and listen. With their permission, ask questions. "How are you holding up?" "I heard your roommate got engaged. How are you feeling about that?" "Your sister's having a baby. I can imagine you're excited and a little jealous of that at the same time." "What's been the hardest part about being single lately?" It will seem invasive. The answers may be hard to hear. But the unmarried man sitting across from you wants nothing more than to be heard. He wants to know that someone cares and can acknowledge that his frustration or pain or annoyance or excitement or whatever he is feeling is real. Just ask. They will talk. I promise.

One last thing: Hug these young men and women. Touch their shoulders. Grab their hands. One of the worst parts of being single can be the lack of physical touch. Especially in the case of those who are praying and working to remain true to God's command regarding sexuality and purity, young singles can go for months without ever knowing the physical care of those who love them and are concerned about them. You don't have to go overboard. Don't be Great-Aunt Gertrude, who kisses their cheeks so hard when they come home at Christmas that they grimace and fall to the floor in a fake faint just to elude you. But do shake his hand. Give her a hug. Let them know, through healthy touch, that they are loved and valued and safe with you.

Pastors and people, you can do this, all of this and more, because you were there once too, even if the circumstances weren't the same. You know what it's like to be alone, but you can be the people, given by God, who keep singles from being lonely.

What hurts the most about being single is not having anyone to share things with; not having anyone who will be there for you no matter what; not having someone to hug you when you've had a rough day, exercise with you, eat dinner with you, go to the store for you when you're sick, sit next to you in church; not having anyone to support you when you're faced with difficult decisions or just be the other half to a pair.

Sure, my family and friends all tell me I can call them whenever I need to or ask them for anything, but what they don't understand is that it's just not the same. There's still a void. I'm still the only one without a significant other at family gatherings, paired with my parents in the family photo while my siblings are with their spouses and children, still the third wheel with all my friends, the only one who is "singled" out by the waitress at the restaurant as she pairs off who is on which bill. Instances like that remind me that I am the odd one out, I am alone, I am single. While everyone else gets to go home with someone, I go home by myself.

Yet there are many great biblical passages that remind me that no matter who is or is not physically by my side in life, God is always with me. He will never leave me. He will never stop caring for me. He will always provide for me.

It also brings me comfort when people acknowledge that being single might be difficult. I don't mean coming up to me and literally saying something like, "I'm sorry you're alone, and I recognize that not having a significant other can be a hard thing to deal with." But I do appreciate little things (which really aren't so little to me), like inviting me over for dinner on a holiday weekend when they know I don't have any family nearby to spend it with or giving me a call or sending a message to say that they're thinking of me. It is comforting just to have someone make time for me so that I'm not spending all of my free time alone.

Sadly, I have never been to a church that does anything to care for singles. There are a few that pray "for those who are single" in the general prayers and a few in which the elderly women are quite active in their attempts to set up any single female they know with any single male they know, based only on the grounds that they are both single and of the opposite sex. But while they have clubs for mothers of preschoolers, clubs for couples, clubs for the retired, the men's group, the women's group, the college group, the youth group (all of which are wonderful and needed), there is nothing for the singles.

This isn't to say churches need a singles club, as this can sometimes be rather awkward and misconstrued as a dating service, but there are ways to care for single people besides forcing them on a date with anyone who is of the opposite sex and breathing. Invite them to dinner. Ask them to sit with you in church. Pray for them. Hug them. Talk to them. Get to know them and help them feel like the church really is their family.

—Madeline, mid-twenties

Widowed

"Dying," one of my seminary professors once told me, "is hard work." And if that is true, grieving the loss of a spouse is downright exhausting. While at Concordia Theological Seminary, I took a class with a fellow student, a young woman in America to study before returning to Europe. She was a nurse, quiet but incredibly insightful.

She told us once about one of her patients, an eighty-year-old man who found out that he was dying from kidney problems and, realizing that it would be a long and painful process, told his doctor he didn't want any surgery to try to fix the problem. The doctors eventually talked him into the surgery, which didn't go well, and he was soon struggling to breathe in the intensive care unit.

Our dear classmate was sniffling as she moved through the story, digging in her pockets for a tissue as she told us that the man's family, upon finding out that he wouldn't recover, told the doctors to take him off his ventilator. Finally, one day while she wasn't working, the doctors purposefully pumped the man full of morphine, slowing down his respiration, and in so doing, deliberately killed the patient.

She was on the verge of tears now, her head bowed, while we sat in a somewhat stunned silence. In that moment, our teacher, a deaconess, taught us a beautiful, Christlike response to her student's need. She didn't simply nod or gloss over the story by moving along to the next topic or simply say, "Oh, thanks for sharing."

Instead, she closed her textbook in silence, turned to her student, and said patiently and quietly, "This still hurts you, doesn't it?" It was exactly the validation our fellow student needed. She started crying, trying to put a voice to her sorrow, saying through her tears that if only she had been working that shift, perhaps she could have saved her patient, that she felt guilt for something outside of her control. I was crying, and so was the woman next to me, and the one next to her, and everyone in the room. Together, as the Church, we learned mutual suffering.

Our instructor calmly appointed one of the students to find a devotion in the *Pastoral Care Companion*

> You do not have to mourn your lost relationships in silence.

that would speak to our friend's situation as a nurse, as one who was not allowed by the law to share the Gospel with any of her patients, as one who had to reconcile that suffering people were killed at the very institution that was supposed to save them. That student began to read Psalm 23 and a passage from Job and then a prayer for comfort, and as she did, our instructor quietly stood up and went to the nurse, standing behind her with her arm on her shoulder while her student sobbed with her hands over her face. When we were finished praying, I went to her, and so did my classmate next to me, and the next, and the next.

This is the way in which we care for our widows and widowers. Human suffering is real, and the way in which Christ comes to His people in its midst is too. That day, our instructor not only showed Christian concern to a student who mattered to her but she also showed us *how*, setting the tangible example in the way in which she cared for her student and immediately recognized her need. And our fellow student taught us something too, letting us get a glimpse into just how difficult it is to care for those you serve, what it means to feel helpless, how to rely only on Christ and His promises for comfort.

We, too, hurt when our widowed friends hurt. We ache with them when they sob in longing for the husbands and wives they've lost. We hold them when they scream out in pain so sharp it can be felt. We stand with them, suppressing our own fears and worries for their well-being, when they panic to the point they feel as though they can hardly draw a breath. We sit in silence with them when they simply can't be alone. That is to say, we are given to show compassion and support to those for whom "until death do us part" is a reality. That is what we, as Christians, do. We come alongside our brothers and sisters in Christ and remind them our Lord uses even suffering to draw us closer and tighter to Him.

In those moments, it is easy for us to grow angry with God, even as we imagine that our widows or widowers are frustrated with Him too. But our Lord always provides a way out, an end to our pain, and an answer to our prayers. "Unexplainable tragedies bring pain and chaos," writes Professor John T. Pless. "God leaves the wound open, to use the words of Bayer. We cry out to God in lamentation in the face of events that defy our capacities for understanding. But the anguished lament ascends from the crucible of faith, not unbelief.

It is a confession of trust in the God who works all things for the good of those who are called according to his purpose (Rom. 8:28). Living in repentance and faith, we are freed from the inward turn of speculation that seeks to investigate the hidden God. Instead, we trust in the kindness and mercy of God revealed in Christ Jesus."[1]

Tertullian, a Church Father writing in the second and third centuries, knew the importance of that kindness and mercy, and he wrote about widows with great warmness. They were, he said, "God's fair ones, God's beloved. With Him they live, with Him they converse, with Him they treat on intimate terms day and night. Prayers are the dowry they bring the Lord and for them they receive His favors as marriage gifts in return."[2] He urged young women to "imitate the example . . . furnished by such women as these and, in your love for things of the spirit, you will bury . . . the flesh."[3]

They are great gifts to us, Tertullian noted—the "sisters of ours—their names are known to the Lord—who, having seen their husbands go to God"[4]—for they permit us to care for them in the Body of Christ, even when we struggle to use the right words and know the right ways to show our love for them. But in so doing, they afford us yet another joy: the reward of seeing the kingdom of God at work. "So it is that the piety of our fellow Christians is a true visible beauty of the church," Dr. Peter J. Scaer wrote. "And this beauty is the reflected beauty of God and the beauty of Christ living and working in and through His earthly family."[5] Their grief over loss is turned to joy, and our uncertainty of how to care for them is given a purpose. God uses one as an example to the other, and the other as a means by which to care for the first. And in so doing, we are all brought into community with one another and, most important, into the arms of Him who would have us kneel at the foot of His cross, receiving from Him "the blessings of Heaven, which last forever."[6]

> I've been a widow for eight and a half years and find it difficult to understand "Why me?" "What is my purpose in life as a widow?" "Whose hearts will I touch?" The first three to four years were the toughest to get through. I reached out for counseling. I needed to be assured it was all right to smile, laugh, and have fun. Now, I have days where I am content being single. I am content to wait, to hope, to be patient.

Having a single Christian support group through the church or the community where men and women with similar feelings can share and explore would have been (and to this day would be) helpful. A Bible study for singles that helps us understand our value in life, coming to know Christ and what He expects from us, and how we can help one another, is another way to remind us we are not alone in being single.

It doesn't help that my church seems to lack a ministry for single women. We all have questions that need to be heard and answered. "Where in the Scriptures do we go for comfort?" "What do we do when the Scriptures don't seem to be helping us anymore? Or is that because we don't understand the Scriptures?" We need the church's help!

—Linda, mid-fifties

Divorced

It shouldn't surprise us that the relationship most affected by the fall into sin in the Garden of Eden—that of the marriage between Adam and Eve—is the relationship that, when broken, hurts and harms our families the most. Divorce is rampant, and promises are disregarded. "As some pastors can testify, some couples who insist on writing their own wedding vows want to replace 'As long as we both shall *live*' with 'As long as we both shall *love*.' "[7] The culture flippantly dismisses marriage with a wave of its hand and lifts up divorce as an easy way out.

But just because it is easy doesn't mean that sin doesn't leave its imprint on the hearts and lives of those whose marriages break apart. Wives hurt, and husbands grieve. Children suffer, and the Body of Christ laments. As the church, we find it difficult to determine how to care for those whose marriage is broken, trying to draw delineations between those who asked for a divorce and those who did not choose their situation, who tried valiantly, who prayed unceasingly, who loved unconditionally, only to have their spouse give up and move on anyway.

Scripture is clear on divorce, and a quick glance through Paul's words in 1 Corinthians 7 can leave the divorced Christian burdened by the Law and desperate for a word of forgiveness from Christ. "I know that I'm sinning by choosing divorce," a friend once told me. "But do I stay and be abused by my husband and watch him abuse our children? Or do I go, protect them, and sin boldly in light of Christ's forgiveness?"

Indeed, He is quick to grant forgiveness for the sake of His Son, whose death wipes clean the slate listing all our sins: "To the Lord our God belong mercy and forgiveness" (Daniel 9:9). And because they are His, they are ours too, just as much ours as they are for those whose marriages have ended.

Pastors, reach out to the divorced husband or wife in your congregation. The wife may have cheated. The husband may be glad to see her go. But both are grieving: for lost love, for lack of companionship, for the guilt and shame they both feel. Declare Christ's forgiveness for them to them, and remind them that they are forgiven for everything—even for divorce.

> Christ is your Bridegroom. You, the Church, are His Bride.

Congregation members, show your fellow brothers and sisters love, whether they were complicit in the breakdown of their marriage or not. Mow the divorced mom's yard. Offer a seat at brunch on Christmas to the man whose wife left him for her boss. Draw them into your families and into your homes. Invite them into your house. Church isn't just a stop-off between home and brunch on Sunday. It's the place where the Lord allows you to receive His Word and Sacrament, and it's also the place where He puts you into proximity with others who need what He has to give just as much as you do. He has given you the grace to care for His beloved children, and you are blessed to be the Body of Christ for them in that place.

To those of you who are divorced, dear brothers and sisters, please let your fellow Christians care for you. Talk to them. Tell them your story and what you struggle with, why Thanksgiving is so hard to deal with now that he's gone and how awful it is to see your daughter only every other weekend and how often you see blessings from your Father's hand despite all the hurt. It will be embarrassing. You will be ashamed to admit that your marriage—promised before God and family—failed. But know that your church family is not out to get you or to make a point. They are simply there to love you through what may well be one of the most traumatic seasons of life you will experience. And they are there to remind you of Christ's forgiveness, which is yours, no matter how hard you fought for your marriage or didn't. Christ is your Bridegroom. You, the Church, are His Bride. That is the marriage that is perfect, truly a match made in heaven. And it is the only one that counts.

Forgiven Even for This

I did not grow up with the understanding that God provides partners. I grew up believing that you go out and find them. We never sat around in youth group talking about how to date or what the purpose of it was. It was just something you did. A guy asks you out, you go, and you have some fun. The end result was not that you would find a person to marry. The point was to check things off of a list. Hold hands, check. Kiss, check. Make out, check. You can see how this progresses.

Sometimes it would progress, sometimes it wouldn't. More often than not, it wouldn't progress if the previously mentioned checkpoints weren't met in a timely manner, leaving you to think that there is something wrong with you or regretting that the checkpoints were met and wondering why this person is a jerk and how did you not see it before?

Society taught me that dating is all about sex. Sex, sex, sex. From what I was able to put together, the person I was "supposed" to marry would just magically appear, and I would know in my heart that this was the right person. As a divorced single, obviously that hasn't worked out.

My fears as a divorced person are fewer than what they were when I was married to my child's father. Do I wonder if I will be alone for the rest of my life? Yes. Do I wonder if the damage I've done to my son by divorcing will harm him in his future relationships with women? Yes. On the other hand, I know that staying with his dad would have been more harmful to him in the long run. At this point, I know that if God wants me to have a husband, He will give me one.

There is a difference between someone in the church who has never been married and someone who is divorced.

It's not easy being alone, especially after enjoying the company of a man for a number of years. When I was a younger woman, it was easy to remedy, at least for a short while. Serial monogamy is not frowned on by the culture. Serial monogamy is a highly stylized term the culture uses to ease the sting of the term *fornication*. Serial monogamy is good, the culture tells you. You're sleeping with only one person who isn't your spouse. Good for you! Easy. Until I got pregnant.

I'm not really a single in the true sense of the word. Single is one. I am two. If I were to be blessed with another husband, he would also need to fill the vocation of father as well. That's a lot to sign up for.
—Marie, late thirties

Celibate

These are blessed people indeed. Those who are celibate live chastely. They are proof that men and women are not animals, that sexual desires *can* be controlled, that lives can be lived fully and in great joy without the constant temptation of sexual relations. That is not to say that these people aren't rare. They are. Celibacy is difficult, even if it is the celibacy that a person maintains while waiting for a spouse, rather than a lifelong undertaking to remain pure both in how a person thinks and in the desires he acts on. Like the rest of us, a celibate person encounters sex at every turn: on television, in magazines, on the Internet, and, well, pretty much everywhere. Temptation is rampant.

Perhaps that's why Paul says in 1 Corinthians 7 that celibacy is a blessing given to some but not to others. "Each has his own gift from God, one of one kind and one of another" (v. 7).

Indeed, "Not everyone can receive this saying, but only those to whom it is given" (Matthew 19:11). There it is again: that gift! "For there are eunuchs who have been so from birth, and there are eunuchs who have been made eunuchs by men, and there are eunuchs who have made themselves eunuchs for the sake of the kingdom of heaven. Let the one who is able to receive this receive it" (v. 12).

That's pretty clear. If the Lord has given you the ability to squelch sexual urges, to steer clear of those temptations that threaten what it means to be a man or a woman at its very core, then blessed are you! Because, given to chastity, you, as a celibate Christian, are free not to worry about the things of this world but to instead put your entire focus on "the things of the Lord, how to please the Lord" (1 Corinthians 7:32). What a gift that is, to devote yourself fully to the things of God. I can think of nothing nobler.

That isn't to say, though, that celibacy is easy. Just because the Lord calls us to an important work doesn't mean He makes the way easy for us. In reality, He never promises us that. He might bless us with a life relatively free from trial, but sometimes He allows it to be just the opposite, even when we are praying to be focused solely on Him.

That's why, as Christians, we acknowledge that we all suffer. Married people suffer. Engaged couples suffer. Those who seem not to be all that bothered by being single suffer. Even those in the Church who have taken to calling themselves *celibrate* instead of *celibate* to remind themselves that there really are joys in leading a life of service to Christ alone suffer.

And yet, joy abounds, because celibacy teaches us that we rely only and wholly on Christ. It teaches us that we have no other options, no other gods, no one else to supply our wants. Celibacy plunks us down directly at the foot of the cross, pointing us back to the only one who can fill our needs.

"Those who live alone, without the companionship and rigor of marriage and sex, are offered an opportunity to realize that it is God who sustains them," wrote Lauren Winner, author of *Real Sex: The*

Naked Truth about Chastity. "Catholic writer Henri Nouwen suggests that this dependence is the unmarried person's primary witness to the married. In singleness, says Nouwen, 'God will be more readily recognized as the source for all human life and activity. . . . The celibate becomes a living sign of the limits of interpersonal relationships and of the centrality of the inner sanctum that no human being may violate.' Unmarried people are asked to specialize in 'creating and protecting emptiness for God,' an emptiness that everyone, married or single, needs to maintain. This, perhaps, is why Aquinas spoke of celibacy as a 'vacancy for God.' In singleness we see not only where our true dependence lies, but also who and what our real family is. Singleness reminds Christians that the church is our primary family."[8]

> There is one who will always answer.

Family members won't always pick up the phone when a celibate single calls. Friends may be busy when he wants to talk. A pastor's schedule may be full when she needs to work through a difficult situation. But there is one who will always answer, always hear and answer, always bless. And that one—the sinless, single Son of God—will always, always be enough, for the celibate, for you, and for me.

THE LORD FULFILLS US

"I know just the girl for you," she said, after a three-minute conversation in which I had introduced myself. Her aged eyes twinkled as she already had me walking down the aisle with this complete stranger. It seemed odd, having just met me, without knowing anything about my likes, hobbies, or thoughts about marriage and family, that she should know the perfect match for me. But I've grown used to this, so taking her hand in a gentle but firm handshake, I said, "Well, thank you. It certainly has been a pleasure meeting you."

I know that people do this because they care. It's out of genuine concern that they see my current state and think I need to be rescued. But that's not necessarily the case. There are a number of wholesome and God-pleasing things that I can do *because* I'm celibate and single. You need to call someone in the dead of the night because of some crisis or nagging worry? A phone ringing in my house will wake only me—and that's not a problem, because I tell people to call whenever they need it (and I mean it). Having a hard day and need someone to grab a cup of coffee after work? My evenings are pretty flexible and I'm always glad to meet with people. Because I live alone, I have more quiet moments throughout the day, during which I can fire off prayers for just about everyone I know as they cross my mind. I have more time to meditate on God's Word, whether through devotions, the writings of the Church's teachers, or straight from the source, because I don't have to worry about pleasing a family.

It's true that sometimes it gets lonely. Sometimes wedding invitations and baby pictures remind me of what the Lord has not chosen to give me at this time. Sometimes, in the static of talk about arranged marriages and distant grand-daughters and the wickedness of single men, it can be hard to believe the Lord's Word that the unmarried and celibate life is good (see 1 Corinthians 7:8, 32–34). But it's during those times that I'm reminded of our Lutheran teaching on vocation. The Lord has placed me in this celibate life, and He's given me plenty to do here. I can be fulfilled, even if it's not in the way that others are—even if it's not in the way others think I should be. I can (and do) rejoice in what He gives others. I love going to weddings and Baptisms and meeting my friends' families. It's what the Lord has given them. But the Lord has given me *this* life, and He daily and richly blesses it with family, friends, teachers, nephews, nieces, godchildren, energy to help when and where I'm needed, time for contemplation, and most important, luxuriant hours of meditating on His Word. It's the Lord who fulfills us, and He does it in the way that He knows to be best.
—Brandon, age 30

Chapter 7

Why You Shouldn't Date Guys with *J* Names and Other Little-Known Facts

By now, you should be realizing that you've got a whole toolkit of dating resources at your disposal. You know what learned pastors throughout history have said about being single. You know what it means to be a man and what it means to be a woman. You know that your Baptism is what matters, not how many boyfriends you've had or girlfriends you've dumped. You know that you're lonely, but that that's different than being alone.

Here's another helpful tidbit: Ladies, don't date guys with *J* names. I dated too many of them: five to be exact. And all of those relationships? Train wrecks, every one. (Good news: train wrecks always make the front page. So that's something.)

All right, so maybe it didn't have anything to do with their names. Or them. Maybe it was mostly me. And a little bit of them. And a lot of the fact that their names started with *J*s. The bigger point is that we, as sinners, are the worst ever at dating. (This just in: I may tend toward exaggeration. Slightly.)

There's a wide range between sleeping with the last person you talked to at the bar and Mom and Dad demanding a blood draw and polygraph from the new guy before he can sit down to dinner. Yet somehow, we stopped believing that you can actually talk to people in order to find out if you like them and started believing that God will instead just drop off the perfect people, marriage-ready, at your doors like a FedEx guy on a delivery route.

We are geniuses at coming up with excuses as to why we shouldn't go out with someone. We are masters at explaining why an hour of conversation and a grande, single-shot, extra hot, light foam latte is just too much to ask.

And the excuses! My goodness, you should hear our excuses. He's too tall. He's too short. She's too quiet. She's too loud. He's not attractive. He's way too attractive. He's not Christian enough. He's too Christian. She's too nice. She's too mean. He sniffs funny. He doesn't sniff funnily enough. She drives a red car. She doesn't drive a red car. He has the personality of oatmeal. He has more personality than oatmeal.

As my pastor once pronounced in a sermon, "Stop. Just stop it."

We really ought to. Because if all the judging and determining and worrying and planning-out-everyone's-entire-future-together-including-who-will-and-won't-be-invited-to-the-wedding-that's-currently-nonexistent weren't frustrating enough, this conversation almost always occurs before the person has ever even (a) met the other person or (b) gone on an actual date.

So, let's consider, just for a moment, this one little thing: Did *a* date—one, single, solitary, lone date—ever kill anybody? Has anyone literally lost a limb over coffee? Have people ever physically melted down over one dinner?

No. Of course not. (Maybe don't check the local police blotter on this, just in case I'm wrong.)

Side note: To be fair, I got pretty close to sawing off my arm once after what was supposed to be a simple dinner out with a guy turned into an eight-hour-long date. Supper turned into a movie that turned into a ball game that turned into ice cream that started to feel like sleep deprivation torture that turned into me practically sobbing, "Please! I'll give you all my credit cards. Just please let me go home!"

Guys, don't keep her there for eight hours. Take her to coffee.

Take her to dinner. If the conversation is good, stay a couple of hours. Then take her home. Let her want to get back together again soon. Don't let the thought "I wonder if I can make a break for it by diving headfirst out that window" cross her mind.

Relationship Rules

Instead, let's assume the state of Illinois gets it right on this one: Date early and date often. All right, don't date early, but feel free to date often. (But not all that often. Let's not go crazy here.)

Instead, let's go with a few quality, deeply theological and profoundly intellectual, criteria:

1. Does he have a debit card?

2. Does she have a pulse?

3. Does she have a car that runs?

4. Will he hurt me?

5. Does his name start with a *J*?

(The correct answers here are (1) He'd better; (2) Gosh, I hope so; (3) Can you settle for a scooter or is this a true deal breaker? (4) Just watch him try; and (5) Run for the hills!)

This is an absurdly long way of saying that dating isn't something to be feared and overanalyzed. It's not the bubonic plague. It will not kill you. You can handle this. Your mom and dad don't need to go on the first date with you. You also don't need to decide how many children you'll have and what their middle names will be before you've even heard his voice.

Of course, you're going to want to make sure he or she has more than the five qualities listed above, but part of meeting up for coffee or going for dinner is to discover just that. Does he go to church? Wonderful. Is he of the same denomination as you? Even better! If not, is he willing to learn? Fantastic.

Does she get along well with her dad? What is his relationship with his previous girlfriends? Is he a hard worker? Is she feminine in how she carries herself and acts toward you? Can the two of you talk comfortably about politics? Does he ask you questions? Does she listen?

> Dating is not the bubonic plague.

These are the kinds of things you can discover during a first date, and if you see potential, they're the same things you get to learn more about over the course of the next five dates or, God willing, the remainder of your life together.

Here's what you shouldn't take away from a first date: He's hot. He's loaded.

The first date itself and any of those subsequent to it can and ought to be about more than what a person looks like or what worldly things he or she brings to the table. It's about a period of time designed to help you learn more about each other's morals and values, to see if the way in which you understand faith and life are in line, to discover if you have mutual and complementary views on family and children, to determine if that person gives more than he or she takes.

You don't have to learn all of this on the first date. (And please, whatever you do, don't fire off question after question like an auctioneer at a job interview. Deep breaths, everybody. Deep breaths!) But if you find that you do have things in common, let the conversation be full and rich as you do move forward. Move steadily beyond the superficial. Don't spend the next three months just talking about the weather. Be purposeful in your conversation, and have fun doing it.

Remember, too, that the person you are walking around the park with today is the same person that you will (if you head that direction) marry. Ladies, repeat after me: You can't and won't change who he is at his core.

Gentlemen, you may change her propensity to leave dirty laundry on the floor. Gals, he may eventually learn to leave his muddy shoes in the garage. But if you are tempted to think, "He's really great, but I just wish he were more open to having kids. Oh, well. I'll con him into wanting babies after we're married," drop whatever you are doing, find yourself a bare wall, and bang your head against it repeatedly until you realize that you are talking nonsense. The man or woman you see is the man or woman you get.

This is not to say that if you are Lutheran and he is Catholic, there is no chance that he may one day want to be catechized in the Lutheran faith as well. It is not to say that if he goes out with the guys every Friday now, he won't stop doing that once you're married to stay home with you instead. But when it comes to the big things, to the way in which he treats you, to the level of importance you hold in his life, to whether he gives selflessly to ensure your well-being, be firmly and acutely aware that those deep-seated ideals are hard to change. And then be equally prepared to have difficult conversations with him or her about those things, no matter the outcome.

Stay Focused Here, Friends

Back to center here: Just so we're clear, going out for coffee isn't a proposal. If you breathe in the same proximity with each other, you're not actually engaged. And if the date is horrible, and you find yourself wishing that your feet were weighted down with cement blocks and that he would toss you in a nearby river, you're really only out a couple of hours that you would have spent pinning gowns to your fake wedding Pinterest board. And you'll have great stories to share with your sisters.

(Oh, the stories I told my sisters. There was the guy who break-danced on his head; the one who asked me to dinner and then bought a pair of two-hundred-dollar cowboy boots to wear that night because he knew I owned some; the one who sat behind me in chapel for weeks while breathing heavily and asking, "Are you ready to let me take you out to lunch yet?" until I was ready to launch myself over the pew, wrap my hands around his neck, and strangle him right there. I could keep this up all week.)

However, there's a flip side to this whole not-taking-dating-so-seriously-that-you've-named-your-kids-before-he's-paid-the-bill thing: Dating also isn't something we take lightly. We don't enter into relationships flippantly or date people because we're looking for something to do. We find a balance in between complete disregard for what it means to be in a relationship and taking things so seriously no one is ever good enough.

Instead, we date because ultimately we're looking for a spouse, for someone that the Lord has chosen uniquely for us. We date because we desire the blessing of marriage, that institution in which a man loves his wife by putting her first and a woman submits to her husband in trust. Dating may be fun, but it is also important. Finding that balance is critical.

Dating for the sake of dating is bad for everybody involved. It cheapens the process by which we learn if this man or woman is the one the Lord has determined in advance for us. It hurts feelings, even if one or both parties claim that it won't. It tells the world that relationships don't matter, that the potential

> We date because ultimately we're looking for a spouse.

joining of hearts and minds and bodies is a toy, something at which we play.

That's why we as Christians don't do one-night-stands or weekend flings. We realize that to understand another person truly and to recognize and appreciate who God has created him to be takes time. Sometimes it takes months. Sometimes it takes years. But any meaningful relationship won't be built on a drink at a club and a taxi ride back to someone's apartment.

We are not so scared or so hard-hearted that we refuse to meet someone. But we also aren't so loose and free that we date everyone all the time, regardless of the way in which it hurts them and ourselves, even if we don't know it.

Finders, Keepers

This gets us to something else: where to find and meet the kind of man or woman who might one day be your husband or wife.

Bad Places	Good Places
Dark alleys	Church
Bathrooms in clubs	Coffee shops
Wiccan chat rooms	Online
A heavy-metal-concert mosh pit	At an event at one of your friend's houses

It's hard to meet Christian singles. (Admittedly, I went through a time when I thought all the single Christian men had been raptured or banished to Area 51.) No one is disputing that. Strangely and sadly, it's even harder to meet them at church, and they certainly aren't beating down your doors when you do meet up. But even if twenty single eligible bachelors just lined up to join your congregation, keep this in mind: Christian men and women exist all over this planet, and while it would be great if the Lord would simply dump off a load of them at your next girls' night out, He may not choose to do that. So be prepared to meet them at church, but also be prepared to meet them through an online dating site or through your friend from work or at a lecture on a topic you both mutually find interesting, such as the rapture or aliens. (No, wait.)

You may also find—swallow hard—that your parents can be helpful in this regard. This is true no matter how old you are, but it's especially a good idea to involve your parents if you are still young (or youngish). My parents, for instance, set me up with their favorite waiter at a restaurant, who turned out to have a baby mama and a set of twin toddlers at home. (Thanks, Mom and Dad. You've been a real help.) So maybe don't ask your parents to follow my parents' example. Still, your mother and father want (or ought to want) what's best for you. It's almost guaranteed that they've been praying for you and for your future spouse since you were young, beseeching the Lord to draw you to a man or a woman He knows is, like Goldilocks, just right for you. Ask your parents if they have friends who have Christian sons or daughters who are single. Question whether there are singles in their church communities. Your parents know you better than almost anyone else. They know what frustrates you and what makes you laugh. They know all your weaknesses—like how you've been known to throw a pan of brownies across the kitchen out of frustration. (Yes, that was me.) They know your greatest gifts, like the way you read to your grandma who has bad eyes and how lovely your voice is in the choir. By God's grace, they can be helpful in introducing you to people of the opposite gender who just may be potential spouses.

Even if your parents don't know any singles, they can play a key role in helping you sort out the duds from the dynamos. When you meet a nice guy or gal, bring them around to your parents' house. Not on the first date. Not in the first week. But if you and Mr. Fabulous are hitting it off, it's good for him to meet your parents and for you to meet his. The way in which he treats his mother, how she interacts with her little brother, if they eat meals together as a family, if or how they do family devotions, all of these things help you discern what kind of man he is, what kind of woman she is, and what the desires of his or her heart are.

Let your parents help you. Let his or her parents help you. Don't, however, include them in every minute part of your relationship. Neither set of parents ought to be allowed to insert themselves into who the two of you are as a couple. That means his overbearing

Italian mother doesn't get to dictate which pizzeria the two of you should go to for dinner; however, getting to know how he interacts with her will go a long way in making sure that the man you are interested in is the same man that the rest of the world—especially his family—sees.

Don't overthink dating. Take it seriously, but don't panic. Meet new people purposefully, but don't sweat it. And while you do, pray. If your heavenly Father has a man or woman in mind for you, He will bring the two of you together in His perfect time. If you are made to wait, He will sustain you. No matter His plan, He has given you freedom in dating. As you experience this unique time in life, enjoy His company, toss back that pumpkin-spice latte, and give thanks to God. He truly is good.

Beware the Unbeliever

Let's take a trip to Theoreticalville. Let's say you meet a great guy. He's thoughtful, gentlemanly, considerate, and opens the car door for you. But let's also say that on the second date you discover he's not a Christian or that he grew up in the church and has since abandoned it. Do you stick it out, praying that the Lord's Word will have its way with him, or do you claim to need to use the restroom, pry the bars off its window, and escape without saying good-bye?

Start by having your pastor on speed dial for this one. He will be an understanding and helpful sounding board in sorting out the best way to handle this kind of situation. He will also likely tell you that just because a man or woman isn't a Christian is no cause to stop returning his or her phone calls or change your name, shave your head, and move to another state.

However, it is a good reason to have almost immediately a very frank and open discussion with this person about the way in which the faith given you by God's grace guides and directs all that you do. It may be awkward or seem too soon, but as a baptized child of God, your very identity is rooted in being one redeemed and marked by Christ in your Baptism. It's like telling the guy you're a daughter or an aunt or a postal worker or a hair stylist. It's who you are. It's what you do. It's how you live. It's what you believe. It's you.

Be understanding, but be firm. Explain that being in church on Sunday is part of your routine; that you desire a spouse who loves the Lord with all his heart and mind as you do; that you expect to raise your children, if God blesses you with them, in a household where family devotions, prayer, and forgiveness abound. If he is open to learning more, if he shows genuine interest in these kinds of holy things, meet up with your pastor. Let him help to explain what it means to be a Christian and begin to answer any questions your friend may have. Pray that the Holy Spirit would be at work in him, moving him to faith in Christ, his Savior from his own demons, from death, from all the gunk and muck the devil would throw at him.

But if your date shows quick and strong disinterest, cut him loose. If he mocks what you believe or argues with you about it, if he rolls his eyes and tells you that religion is for losers, part ways. If he says he loves you but that you'd be the one who would raise your children in the church, not him, it's time to pay real and careful heed to Scripture's warning that we ought "not be unequally yoked with unbelievers" (2 Corinthians 6:14).

It will be hard in the moment. What attracted you to him in the first place may seem like enough to start to build a relationship on, but it isn't. A part of you, even if it's small, will arise and try to convince you to keep quiet about your faith since it may offend the other person. Tertullian noted that we too often "practice tolerance" and that that tolerance is "the price of their silence."[1] You don't need to be silent or tolerant of beliefs that are untrue and unfounded.

The faith is yours. Christ has put it in your heart and on your lips. You know what you believe. You know how to speak about it. If you try to start a discussion with your significant other about Christ and what life as a Christian looks like, only to find that the words aren't coming out the way they're supposed to or even not at all, use the church's historic creeds. Let them be your guide. They remind of you what you believe and give voice to what you confess. "I believe in God, the Father Almighty. . . . And in Jesus Christ, His only Son, our Lord. . . . I believe in the Holy Spirit, the holy Christian Church, the communion of saints, the forgiveness of sins, the resurrection of the body, and the life everlasting." (Can someone get a Staples button and a "That was easy!" in here?)

The only thing upon which a relationship can find firm footing is Christ. Without that, nothing is sure. Not your future, not his. If there is the

> Don't overthink dating, and don't panic.

potential for marriage and children, those will be based on shaky, shifting ground as well.

Not settling is hard. The temptation as a single person is to think that you're better off married and a little unhappy than to be single and a little unhappy. Sometimes waiting for the right person seems downright pointless, especially when our minds and hearts tell us that we would rather be someone, anyone, than be alone. But your Lord tells you otherwise. He tells you not to bind yourself to someone who disregards Him, not only for your benefit but also for the man or woman to whom you would be responsible.

Do the hard work now. Separate out the men and women who are on the same page as you like a cowboy sorting cattle on the Montana Hi-Line. It's worth it, because relationships and marriage and children and long lives together are gifts from our heavenly Father, meant for our benefit and blessing and good. So start out on the right foot, walking together in the one who created the two of you for each other: in Christ.

✳✳

THESE ARE NOT THE DATING WEB SITES YOU WERE LOOKING FOR

When it comes to online dating, there are two simple things to consider. Number 1: Online dating is not sketchy. Number 2: There are a lot of sketchy people online. I was, I mean, *my friend* was an anti-online-dater for a long time. It seemed like a last-ditch, desperate measure. It was for old people and gamers, not for healthy, vibrant, in-their-prime twenty-somethings. But when I, I mean, *my friend* learned firsthand that men can actually date two girls at one time without either woman ever knowing about the other, it's weird how quickly *a person* can decide that she never wants to meet anyone in real life ever again. I mean, theoretically.

If something like that were to have happened to me, I would have dished out the money for one of the popular dating sites and grumpily sat back to prove to the world that this kind of thing didn't work. If it were me.

The first few guys didn't work. One only talked about himself. One was Christian but wasn't the same denomination as me. One was roughly two feet shorter than me. (Hey, tall girls think this way. We want our husbands to protect us, not us to protect our husbands.) And then, out of the blue, I met my future husband. We figured out within a few messages that we were both Lutheran and that we both held the same things dear: hymnody, the Lutheran Confessions, worship. Then we discovered we were both farm kids; I grew up on a pig farm, and he's a dairyman. We both love cowboy boots and being outside and country music. He was handsome, winsome, and funny.

We started e-mailing each other almost every day; he'd write me in the morning and I'd send him a message every night before I went to bed. He didn't pressure me to meet him. He took his time. It was clear he wanted me to be and feel comfortable before we ever met in person. And that made me want to meet him all the more. His messages made me laugh—out loud—and it was obvious he was taking a genuine interest in who I was as a person.

When we did agree to meet, he drove three hours through the worst blizzard in Missouri that year to have coffee with me. He arrived at the coffee house where were supposed to meet, only to find it closed due to the weather. He tried another. Also closed. And then a third. We eventually ended up meeting at the mall, sitting in the midst of shoppers while we sipped Starbucks. That was March. In July, he proposed. In November, we got married.

That's the way that online dating can, in a nearly perfect world, work. By being prayerfully deliberate, you can meet a godly man or woman as easily online as you can in person, even as you must be careful to guard whom you trust. That is to say, men are supposed to treat women with as much respect online as they are expected to treat them in person. Women are to be as genteel and feminine online as they would be in real life. It means that, if you are game for trying online dating, you don't act in a dishonest fashion online, just as you wouldn't be misleading in person. You don't upload pictures of yourself when you were fifty pounds lighter or before you had gray hair. You don't say that you're an oil tycoon when you're still in grad school. (Unless, of course, you're an oil tycoon who's still in grad school.) You're real, as real online as you are with your best friends who hang out with you on Friday night. Relationships hinge on honesty, and even though the Internet allows more leeway when it comes to this, you as a Christian are held to a higher standard, a better way.

It's also important to take your time when it comes to online dating. (That, by the way, requires some patience. Don't give up in a hot minute because God didn't drop a Banana Republic male model out of the sky and into the driver's seat of your turquoise Elantra.) You are in control of the situation; you get to call the shots with regard to how fast or slow you get to know someone. Just because a man asks for your phone number in his first message to you doesn't mean you need to provide it. Wait for a man of God who understands his place in relation to you and vice versa; he'll take his cues and pace from you, doing his best to make sure that you're comfortable first, putting your needs in front of his.

These instances provide a brilliant opportunity to be faithful to who you are as a child of God, even over the Internet. You don't need to rush into anything. You can e-mail for a month before you meet for a drink. You can talk on the phone for another month if that's what you need. Finding a girlfriend isn't tantamount to an Olympic sprint. You both may decide fairly quickly that you're just right for one another, but usually it takes some time and work to get to that point. So if the woman with whom you're talking starts to pressure you, tell her you're uncomfortable with the speed in which she's trying to move and offer her the opportunity to slow down. Chill. Breathe. Pray.

What Love Is

What should love look like, according to God? God says our love should be patient, kind, not jealous, not boastful, not proud, not rude, not self-seeking, not easily angered, no recorder of wrongs, not delighting in evil, rejoicing with the truth, always protecting, always trusting, always hoping, always preserving (1 Corinthians 13:4–8). . . .

Our values, the desires of our hearts, should reflect what God wants and knows is best for us. Internet dating can help us place those values clearly up front, but *only* if we know these values ourselves.[2]

Dear Sexting, You're No Good

There's one more thing: Don't send compromising pictures of yourself, either over the Internet or via text message. Men and women alike will ask for and expect that kind of behavior online, and you, in faith, are given to resist that temptation, because no matter how pious you are or how faithful you can be in church attendance or reading your Bible, it *will* be a temptation. As sinners, our desire is always to be liked. Our egos cry out for it. The thought of being praised for our rugged jaw lines or our curvaceous bodies or our willingness to give in to the perversion of those who simply want us at face value will be hard to overcome.

But it is possible to overcome it. The Lord will and does provide a way out. You are His beautiful daughter, His handsome son. You matter to Him, and He loves you. He doesn't want to see you in pain, and allowing yourself to be treated in this way will hurt you. He wants instead for you to have only the best, and the best is exactly what He gives you! His plan for you to have what is good and right for you is the reason that He places you into families with parents and siblings who can care for you in your singleness, into congregations with pastors and fellow Christians who can remind you that your true hope is in Christ alone, in groups of friends and communities who can understand your struggles and love you through them.

So if you do slip up, if you behave online in a way unbecoming a lady or a gentleman, if you fib a little about who you are or send pictures you ought not send, if you blur the lines about what makes you you so that a guy will like you, or if you exaggerate your best qualities to get a girl to give you her much sought-after number, know that, like a father who runs to a child who has fallen and skinned his knee, so your Father comes to you, eager to scoop you up in His arms and care for you in the best and most tender of ways. He will bathe you again and again in His Word, in that which slashes your sins to pieces and burns all your lustful thoughts and poor behavior to the ground. As your Good Samaritan, He will bind up all the hurts of your past relationships, all your shame over mistakes made and poor decisions, all the fears and worries about your future and the man or woman you may or may not share it with. And then, in His mercy, He will forgive you for all of it.

Online dating isn't just for the desperate. It can be, when used properly and in healthy ways, a great tool for slowly and calmly getting to know a person who has the potential to be someone important and dear to you. Use it that way. Pray for discernment. The Lord hears, and He will answer.

✳✳

WHEN THE PERFECT RELATIONSHIP—ONLINE OR NOT— DOESN'T WORK

Breakups stink. Broken relationships—no matter how new or deeply rooted—hurt. We experience defeat and failure. We are frustrated that yet another friendship didn't work out the way we'd planned. We feel sad, sorry that we're hurting someone else and sorry that we ourselves hurt. And we know pain, which reminds us that we are sinners who have said unkind things and acted in anger; we have looked for the worst in others instead of putting the best construction on them; we have acted selfishly, treating people in our lives as if we mattered more than them. They humble us too. Even when we see them coming, even if they are good for us, they cut deeply for a time. When we don't see them coming, they take our breath away with alarming speed.

There's no easy way to tell another person that you need to part ways. You simply do it. You are honest and forthright without outlining every single nuanced detail about why your relationship simply won't work. As a Christian, you are to look out for the other person, especially in those moments. You undoubtedly bear in yourself an unending list of grievances and annoyances; giving voice to those may relieve your guilt and frustration. But are they helpful? Are they true? Are they said in love to the betterment of the other person? Not usually. And so we hold them in and share them with our pastor or our parents or our friends who can listen, reminding us that we have sinned in relationships too.

Likewise, there's no easy way to hear from another person that your time together is finished. We innately want to beg and plead, to promise that it will be different if we're given another chance, to swear that we can do better. Sometimes relationships do simply need a readjustment or alignment, like a chiropractor cracking a bone back into place. But most times, our cajoling is pointless. The other person has made up his mind. He's finished, and he's through. We have the opportunity to respect his decision graciously, stepping aside when we're asked to.

We pray then, sometimes with tears that soak the shoulder of our mother's sweatshirt and sometimes with tears that mingle with water in the shower, running down the drain, never noticed by anyone else. We pray for mercy, and our Lord gives it to us. We pray for peace, and He bestows it. We pray for this cross to be removed, and it is. But it is all done in His timing, and His ways are not ours. If He allows us to suffer, we do so in faith, confident that He is forming us through this experience to trust only in Him. If He lessens the pain quickly, we receive that in faith too, thankful that He has delivered us by His grace.

We grieve. We mourn the loss of a friend and a confidant, no matter how crazy or awful or wonderful that person may have been. We suffer in what feels like complete silence, except for the ticking of the clock or the hum of the refrigerator as we sit alone and quiet in our pain. The world offers no comfort, no answers, no closure, no sound. We struggle to figure out how to cope, how we'll get out of bed the next day, how we'll show our face in public.

It's all in vain. We cannot pray enough, fast enough, cry enough, or beg enough. And we don't have to. Christ has already done that for us. He has asked the "Why?" question and answered it too. He is a fit Bridegroom for us. He is not selfish. He makes no demands. He does not walk away once or twice or ever. He loves, and He is love.

He comforts us, even as He is comfort. He has committed Himself fully to us. He is trustworthy, loving us as we are: imperfect and flawed. He puts us first in everything. He suffers on our behalf. He protects us, keeps us, and loves us.

You do not have to mourn your lost relationships in silence. Open the curtains. Look to the sun. The heavens are not closed. The Lord does hear. He will answer. He has already.

✳✳

FACEBOOK IS RIGHT: IT'S COMPLICATED

Whenever I speak on being single, there is always one young woman who inevitably asks, "I just broke up with my boyfriend, but I still really like him. We just get along so well! Can we still be friends?" And inevitably I make her cry by saying, "Not really, no." Relationships are hard. Breakups are harder. Reverting back to platonic friendship is hardest. It very rarely works. Instead, couples break up, keep talking, and then either end up back together and then apart again (in a painful, awful cycle) or horribly jealous when one of them moves on with a new guy or gal. (There are exceptions to this rule. Of course there are. There always are!) (In addition to this, you will drive your friends crazy. Because *Be strong in faith and fervent in love* although they love you, they hate watching you go back into a situation that's no good for you time and time again. And if there's one group of people you need not to hate you at a time like this, it's your best friends.)

It's helpful to talk with the other person about how your relationship will or won't look. (Maybe it's not best to have that discussion in the heat of the moment when one is crying and the other is trying to make a beeline for the door so he can pick up his next date for dinner.) But do be purposeful in requesting or finding a time to talk through whether you'll remain in contact, what that contact will or won't include, and the frequency of it.

After my first engagement fell apart, I talked to my fiancé only twice. I called him that night to see if he was okay. (Although now that I think about it, *he* broke up with *me*. Who was supposed to be calling whom there?) And I said, "Thank you," when he dropped off a box of stuff I'd given him. That was it.

Then, in one fell swoop and in a fit of unprecedented mental strength, I unfriended him from Facebook and deleted all his e-mails. I knew it had to be done swiftly and decisively or I'd be bawling over them like a three-year-old every Friday night for the next year. Somewhere in the fog of lost love, I knew it was best.

And it was. There was no way I could check up on him, no way I could send an e-mail in a weak moment, no chance of making a phone call when I had been crying for hours. It worked. He was out of sight, and I had no choice but to plow forward.

So maybe you have to unfollow your ex-girlfriend on Twitter. Perhaps you'll have to delete her number out of your phone for a while. You may have to ask your friends not to talk about her for a few months or to alert you if she's going to be at the same function as you. It will be difficult. This woman has been your person for the past several months—maybe even years. She's the first one you'll want to call when you need to talk or something goes wrong. It will be hurtful and hard not to make her your first line of defense.

Nevertheless, time and space are good. They heal hurts and close wounds. As the days and months pass, your heart will heal. You may be interested in meeting another person again. You may not want to go on a date for a year. You will not suffer alone, though. "For as we share abundantly in Christ's sufferings, so through Christ we share abundantly in comfort too" (2 Corinthians 1:5). He will never cut off contact with you. You are His, and He will not let you be moved to despair. He has provided a way out of the pain by giving you His words of comfort, His body and blood for forgiveness, His pastors, His church.

Here's one last, delightful nugget: When relationships get you down (or up), when your boyfriend or girlfriend hurt you and you are having a difficult time seeing your way through the pain, you don't have to show up to church bouncing off the walls like a kid at the McDonald's PlayPlace. You can go to church sad, miserable, and frustrated. You can go to church missing your boyfriend. I glared at my pastor through one entire sermon because of a bad breakup. (He noticed, for what it's worth, and yours probably will too.) What the Lord has to give you isn't dependent on your attitude or your emotions. He will provide you with the comfort and the peace you need, no matter your mood. He is faithful. He cares about you. It will not always hurt this bad. He loves you, and He will not fail.

Guilt over Joy

However, this isn't the only way that relationships complicate life. Things get muddled up when relationships go well, when they progress as God intended for them to, when they grow and flourish in His grace. Should the Lord bless you with a godly girlfriend who becomes your fiancée who is then your wife, you may find that your unmarried friends will find this a hard pill to swallow, not because they aren't thrilled for you but because they are grieving for themselves.

That leaves you—and them—in a difficult position. You feel guilty for your joy, while they remain frustrated at their lack of it. Suddenly, you are "one of them," the people who don't understand the single life, even though you've lived it up until that moment. Your options are few: either don't talk about your girlfriend/fiancée/spouse, or do talk about her while simultaneously acknowledging that your friends' burdens are still real and difficult to bear.

As a newly engaged woman, I was eager to talk to my girlfriends about my wedding dress and who would be a bridesmaid and why we were choosing to cut a pie instead of a cake. But I also realized that conversations like that would make my single gal pals, while excited, feel pain, even if it was slight. I knew this because I'd been on the receiving end of it. I'd been the one who put on the most real phony smile you've ever seen and squealed in a convincingly excited way every other time someone announced an engagement, a wedding, or a baby. And while my joy for my married friends had always been honest and genuine, it also always coincided with a longing to have what they had: a spouse. This longing soured, if only in part, my excitement for them.

So if the Lord plants Mr. Right in the midst of your life, be mindful of those who have not yet been given such a blessing. Share your joy, but don't rub it in. Temper it for the sake of your fellow brothers and sisters, keeping in mind their hurts and the prayers they offer for a relationship akin to the one the Lord has given you. Yes, "Be kind to one another, tenderhearted, forgiving one another, as God in Christ forgave you" (Ephesians 4:32).

If you are dating or engaged or married, be an advocate for those who are still single. Assure them that you understand. Acknowledge that what they are feeling—whether it is indifference or fear or sadness or anger—is real and that it is okay. Encourage them to talk to you when they need someone simply to listen. Remind them that you have been where they are and felt what they feel. Pray alongside them: "Wait for the LORD; be strong, and let your heart take courage; wait for the LORD!" (Psalm 27:14).

Christ-centered relationships can be the cause of pure delight, but they can also create tension between friends. Be open with your friends. Be strong in faith and fervent in love. Be honest with one another. Be in prayer. The Lord hears, and He will answer.

CRYING FOR A GODLY HUSBAND: A NOTE TO THE LADIES

Wifehood and motherhood are the scriptural norms for womanhood. Woman was created for the man. When Scripture talks about women's roles and identity, it is in relation to the man. This is how God set it up. When and where wifehood is absent, we are dealing with a case of an exception. It is possible that such a case is exceptional in a positive sense, like when Paul describes chastity as the higher or greater gift. Where a woman is content to be single and does not desire marriage, she is blessed! But many times, *most* times even, a single woman is exceptional (outside the norm) in a "this is a sad, broken, fallen world" way. A woman may not be a wife because she's divorced or widowed. These are sorrowful realities. Or in some cases, a woman may be yet (or even perpetually) unmarried while longing, hoping, and praying for a godly spouse. This is a cause of sorrow. It is okay to talk about it this way. It is all right to acknowledge that being single can be a gift (those given the higher gift of chastity) but that it can also be, and more often is, a burden to bear. Before marrying, I cried for a godly husband that I did not have. When I stopped pretending to love the independence, I whimpered on a good night and wailed on a bad. While not at all the same, it could very carefully be compared to a childless wife. There is nothing wrong with her grief over her barrenness. That deep grief acknowledges that she bears a burden on account of having been excluded from the good, blessed gift of motherhood. When a woman is excluded from the good, blessed gift of wifehood, it can be said just that plainly. I struggled with coveting the lives, vocations, and gifts of those women who were married mothers. Covetousness is a bad thing, but desiring God's good gift of marriage is a natural, positive thing. It's not a sin. It was hardwired into us from the beginning. [Regarding the joy of meeting her husband while still caring for her single friends:] Did I feel guilty? Yes. Not because I'd done something wrong, obviously, but because it felt wrong to enjoy something so wonderful when others were deprived. It felt like going home to eat as much as I wanted after spending the day in the slums of Caracas with people who were starving. It's an awful feeling. It can't be made right, but it can be handled rightly by calling a thing what it actually is. Being single is (almost always) sad. It is normal for women who desire the gift of marriage to feel sad if they don't have it. It is good to pray to the Lord and ask for this blessing. I felt sad when I was single. That's just a fact. I felt sad. Then, when I got engaged, I worried about making my still-single friends sad. Remember that if they desire marriage, they are probably already sad, whether or not their friends are engaged. That being said, there is a certain element of lemon juice on a paper cut going on here. You are good to be sensitive in this way. I also tried to be sensitive. Once I got engaged and married, I didn't pretend that I loved being single. I didn't love it. Being single made me sad. I felt sad and I prayed for that gift of marriage night and day. There was a constant undercurrent of sadness and praying and praying and sadness. Repeat, repeat, repeat, along with some sin tossed in there because I'm a sinner. It is better to share the burden of a single woman by acknowledging that it *is* a burden rather than saying things such as, "Oh, well; you have lots of other good things going for you!" Sure, being single has its perks. We both know that. But I would never trade them for the immense joy and blessing of marriage. Why pretend? Commiserate. Show love. Be compassionate. Pray for them. Care for them. Share God's Word with them. I was the first of my college girlfriends to marry [and] I felt like I was somehow rubbing it in their faces to be happy. It was awkward and hard. I wanted to be happy but not too happy because my Happy might be another person's Sad. But the good friends shared in my joy just as willingly and readily and sincerely as I shared in their sorrow. That is what we are called to as Christians: both to rejoice and also to mourn. I hope that is helpful. Your dear friends will know that you feel their pain, and you will know it because the Lord works in you to produce things such as love, joy, peace, patience, kindness, goodness, faithfulness, gentleness, and self-control.

—Marissa, early thirties

Chapter 8

Love > Sex

So if you men now know what it means to be a man, while you women realize what it means to be a woman, how do you hold yourself together (read: not give into the devil's fib that sex outside of marriage is a good thing) until the Lord gives you a spouse?

The culture isn't going to help you in this regard. It's going to encourage you to choose your own morality rather than relying on Christ and on His Word. It's going to tell you that anything goes, that if something feels right it can't be wrong, that your pastor and your church and your Lord and His Commandments have no business telling you what you can and can't do. It's your body, after all!

Ha-ha. That's funny. *Your* body. As though you created it and redeemed it! (Sorry to be such a killjoy, but you didn't.) Actually, your body isn't really yours at all. "Or do you not know that your body is a temple of the Holy Spirit within you, whom you have from God?

You are not your own, for you were bought with a price. So glorify God in your body" (1 Corinthians 6:19-20).

According to the National Campaign to Prevent Teen and Un-planned Pregnancy, 81 percent of those who claim a religious affiliation between ages 20-29 aren't aware this is the case, because 81 percent of those who claim a religious affiliation admit to having had premarital sex: a shocking figure.[1] But we have given into this. We haven't taken our Lord at His Word in the Sixth Commandment when He bids us to lead a sexually pure and decent life, when He tells us that sex is meant for marriage. Even if we are still virgins, we certainly haven't maintained pure thoughts. That's for sure.

"The idea of virginity is not popular in the worldly world," wrote Thomas Dubay. "What was formerly referred to as a woman's honor has . . . become almost a dishonor. It is often considered as a deprivation at best, an illness at worst."[2] That change is part of why we have a frightening number of men who have slept with or had relationships with women to the point that they are numb to knowing what they should be looking for in a potential wife. On the flip side, women sleep with as many partners as they want, dress however they want, engage in completely unfeminine behavior that would give our grandmas a heart attack, all in the hopes that a guy will turn his head. It's even taught our future wives and mothers that it's okay to abort their own children. Lord, have mercy!

The culture has told us that this behavior will bring us joy, that we'll feel free, that we'll be more ourselves than we've ever been before. Instead, in actuality, our culture is more hardened than ever, our women know less and less the joys of being a wife and mother, and our men grow increasingly callous to the hurt and suffering that superficial relationships create instead.

So here's something a little daring, a little scandalous: Commit to no sex outside of marriage. That's probably not what you wanted to hear. It's difficult. Sometimes, it just downright stinks. It doesn't feel fair. Trust me. I waited twenty-nine v-e-r-y l-o-n-g years.

But know this: The Lord has given us the commandment for our own protection, for our own good. He's given it to us to keep us from hurting and from being hurt.

> So glorify God in your body.

This or That

Scenario 1: You meet a guy. ("Hi, guy.") He's cute and smooth. ("Hey, girl.") He's charming and flirty. (I can't keep this conversation up forever.) He wants your number. You go to dinner, and he buys you a couple of drinks. He tells you you're beautiful. He shuts the car door for you and drives you back to his place. And just as you think you ought to head to the bathroom to text your best friend, "OMG! I think he's the one!" he's got you on his bed, your blouse is on the floor, and he's unzipping your pants.

But he loves you. And it's different with you than it is with everybody else.

Of course it is. Just as different as it was with the last three girls he told that to.

You can keep telling yourself that, but that's not what love is, and he's not treating you the way a future wife—a woman made in God's image—is to be treated. Instead, he is to uphold you in all things, but especially in this: "The virgin's role is directly pointed to a loving communion with the Lord himself. Her vocation lies at the core reality of the *ekklesia*, the biblical 'one thing' to gaze on the beauty of the Lord."[3]

The problem is that a lot of men and women don't understand sex and relationships and the way in which God would have them work. That's just one reason why it would be great if every date or relationship came with one of those gigantic red warning lights that goes off in cartoons, the kind that are accompanied by eardrum-rupturing sirens and a set of gigantic, bugged-out, cartoon eyes. Because right after he shut the car door and you headed back to his place, those lights would have gone off with such gusto the lunar rover could have seen them in space.

Scenario 2: You meet a guy. ("Hi, guy.") He's cute and smooth. ("Hey, girl"—and so on.) He's charming and flirty. He wants your number. You go to dinner, and he buys you a couple of drinks. He tells you you're beautiful. He shuts the car door for you . . . and drives you home. He walks you to the door and thanks you for the time you took to spend the evening with him. He tells you he really enjoys your company, that he appreciated learning more about you and is anxious to meet up again sometime if you're game for it. You go inside, take off your shoes, and sit down on the edge of your bed.

Your phone dings. He's texted you, checking to make sure you made it in safely and wishing you a good night. You stare at the screen, wondering if he's for real. And guess what? He is.

Sex on date 1 is bad. So is sex on date 1,001. There's no place, no time, no way that sex is right before you get married. There just isn't.

It's difficult to hear that there's no easy way out, that we may have feelings we can't act on, especially when "Celibacy is seen by almost everyone as a surrender, a giving up of 'sex' and marriage."[4] But we're not animals. We can and do discipline our bodies. Contrary to what every pop song says, we actually don't have to act on every feeling or urge our body knows. We can wait. We can hold out.

Sex within the bounds of marriage is rich and rewarding. Marriage binds men and women together holistically. Their hearts are joined in love. Their minds think and act in service to and on behalf of the other person. Even their bodies are united. And that love only multiples and gets better with time. My dad, to this day, tells my sisters and me how much he loves our mother. "Girls," he'll say with a look of wonder in his eye, "I love this woman! Man alive, do I love her." And I believe him, despite the fact that his proclamations of love for my mom totally used to gross me out as a child. Now, as an adult, I know without a doubt that he actually loves her more than the day he married her. She's got his back, and he has hers. They've been together through surgeries, cancer, and deaths in the family. There's nothing she doesn't know about him, and he knows everything about her. And still they continue to talk, to work on their relationship, to forgive each other, and to receive from Christ all the good things He gives in marriage.

To those of us who are single, it sounds ideal. Do what the Lord says. Wait for marriage. Suffer silently when your doctor asks you if you're sexually active and then gives you the hairy eyeball when you say you aren't. Stay quiet when co-workers talk about their latest sexual exploits. Endure.

The Kicker

Then there's the little secret no one ever tells you (that is, after all, the purpose of a secret): Evangelical Christianity will tell you that because you waited to have sex until you got married, because you obeyed God and listened to His will, that when you do put a ring on your husband's or wife's finger, the sex will be mind blowing. Cataclysmic. Earth shattering. Wall pounding.

Well, maybe. But maybe not. That's not a promise the Lord has given you. The Small Catechism bids us to "lead a sexually pure and decent life in what we say and do, and husband and wife love and honor each other" (Sixth Commandment). It doesn't say, "Lead a sexually pure and decent life in what you say and do, and your wife will swing from the chandelier in red stilettos every night!" It says that when you're married, you and your spouse will love and honor each other. The end.

Because you know what? Love and honor are what matters. They count. Love and honor founded in Christ are enough to sustain a marriage. Sex, whether before or after, isn't. It's a beautiful gift, to be sure. It's the means by which "a man as husband reveals to the woman what it is to be a woman, and the woman as wife reveals to the man what it is to be a man."[5]

However, a Christ-centered marriage isn't about sex alone. Certainly, it includes it as one of the amazing ways that Christ joins His children together in holy matrimony, but it isn't the only thing.

No one can force you to hold onto your virginity until your wedding night. Nobody's policing bedrooms to see if you're waiting or not. In fact, "There have been many good men who tried very hard to subdue the body, and yet made little progress" (Apology of the Augsburg Confession XXIII 20). But also know this: "Premarital sex is a hypocritical act. It is a fake. A physical saying of that which is not."[6]

So, go ahead: Look forward to marriage. Look forward to sex! But look forward to it. Wait. Pray for patience. Take cold showers. Look away from pictures or people that tempt you. Guard that which you can only give to your husband or wife once. "For the grace of God has appeared, bringing salvation for all people, training us to renounce ungodliness and worldly passions, and to live self-controlled, upright, and godly lives in the present age" (Titus 2:11–12).

Kind of a Big Deal

Virginity is a big deal; so big, in fact, the Holy Spirit inspired the author of Judges to write about the pain that comes from losing it. Jephthah, a leader of Israel and at war with the Ammonites, promised the Lord that "whatever comes out from the doors of my house to meet me when I return in peace . . . shall be the Lord's, and I will offer it up for a burnt offering" (Judges 11:31). And that was all well and good until Jephthath's daughter was the one to meet him at the doors of his house. His daughter didn't ask her father to go back on his vow, to spare her from death. She didn't freak out and blame her dad for ending her life too young. Instead, she asked one thing of him: "Leave me alone two months, that I may go up and down on the mountains and weep for my virginity" (v. 37). And so she goes, mourning for two solid months over that which was lost.

> Virginity is a big deal.

Your virginity—your sexuality—is that important. It is worth protecting and treasuring, worth grieving over when it is lost to someone who is not your husband or wife. But the Lord does not stand idly by while you search frantically for ways to guard His gift to you. Instead, He gives you the gift of prayer and of honesty, both of which He uses to protect you and your heart.

1. Pray

(You really should have seen that one coming.) Tell the Lord what you struggle with in terms of your sexual desires. Ask Him to keep you steadfast in His Word, in that which bids you to wait.

When the devil whispers sweetly in your ear, "She's a beautiful woman. And she really, really likes you. What does it hurt to slip into the shower with her? You won't let anything happen. You can stop anytime you want to," pray the Lord's Prayer. And pray it out loud. Let God's words be on your lips. "Submit yourselves therefore to God. Resist the devil, and he will flee from you" (James 4:7).

Before getting out of bed in the morning and before falling asleep at night, pray:

> *O Lord, who directs our lives day after day, I thank*
> *You that You have so graciously led me through*

the days of my youth and have preserved me from straying and falling. I come to You for special guidance in these days when I am choosing a life companion. Lord, look down the pathway of my life, and if this woman (man) is truly a fitting partner and companion for me, then grant that our lives may be fused into one and that we may journey on together happily.

Keep me pure in heart. Grant that I may do nothing against Your commandments and offend You. Grant that my conduct may faithfully reflect that I am a child of God.

O Lord, if it be Your will, grant that we may understand each other better from day to day and love each other sincerely. Above all, give us the grace to keep You in our hearts as our friend and guide. I ask this for the sake of Jesus, my Lord and Savior. Amen.[7]

2. Talk about Sex

If you're dating someone now, talk about sex. It's all right. In fact, it will clear the air and make what seems so secretive and mysterious less scandalous. Be open with the man or woman you're dating about the difficulties of keeping our Lord's commandment. Discuss ways to keep yourselves from situations that may make it easy for you to stumble, such as going on dates that involve hanging out with other friends or staying out of your bedroom when you're alone together. When your boyfriend is on top of you on the couch, and the devil hisses, "Just relax; it doesn't matter where he's touching you, because you love each other," stop everything. Move apart. Repent, and ask your heavenly Father for forgiveness.

Set boundaries. But be careful that you don't create boundaries only to enjoy the loopholes that go along with them. In Lauren Winner's book *Real Sex,* she encourages couples not to do anything prior to marriage that they wouldn't be willing to do on the steps of the Capitol building.[8] That works in theory, but there's a lot of, um, "unique" people out there willing to do a lot of things in front of a lot of other people.

That, of course, is the beauty of the way in which Luther explains the commandment regarding sexuality. He doesn't say, "You can do *X* and *Y* and *Z* as long as you are fully clothed." He describes a way of living, a manner in which you exist in the world, an attitude. So, set limits, but don't make them in such a way that you can find ways to break them without feeling badly about it.

You can also (gasp!) talk to your pastor. It will be awkward. You'll blush and feel like it's the end of the world and that he will be horrified to hear what you have to say. (I promise that—unless you are missing your soul—you'll feel that way. That's all there is to it, so you might as well get over it now.) That's the bad news. The good news is that your pastor actually won't be scandalized. He's a living, breathing human being too, which means he understands and empathizes. The better news is that your pastor will give you Jesus. You can confess your sins to him, and he will absolve you with Jesus' forgiveness right there, personally, for you. And there's nothing to feel ashamed about in that.

If you're not dating someone, it doesn't mean you're off the hook when it comes to being mindful of what you're feeling and thinking. Pornography is rampant and free, and you can hardly flip through television channels without seeing somebody climbing into bed with somebody else. So, even now, while you are single, see number 1. And then, if God blesses you with a boyfriend or girlfriend, see number 2. Again.

While you wait, ask your friends for help. Ask them to keep you from situations that will cause you to fall into temptation or sin. Ask them to be on call when you are feeling particularly prone to giving in to this temptation. Ask them to pray to our Lord on your behalf.

3. Repent

If you've already slipped up, repent. Receive the Lord's forgiveness for you. Go to your pastor. Confess your sin to him, and let him speaks God's words of peace and forgiveness directly to you. Bask in His grace and mercy, in the knowledge that He does not hold your sins against you. Remember that your sins are removed, that He remembers them no more.

This doesn't mean that you won't remember them, though. Sex, after all, is meant to draw you closer to the other person, and it does just that. The hormones released in sex are the same ones released in childbirth; they're God's way of binding you to that person (or baby) forever, for life. So when you have sex with someone who isn't your husband or wife, and even when you feel remorse and repent of it, you will undoubtedly, at least for a time, still feel a connection to that person, one that makes it awfully hard to forget him or her and move on.

In those moments—in all moments—live in Christ's mercy, and under the grace of Christ resolve to life a chaste life. Stand firm in this conviction, because there is hope in the midst of all this hurt and pain. There can be, believe it or not, even joy, whether you've stumbled and given in to the desires of your flesh or whether you're holding out. That hope, that joy, is Christ. Christ has forgiven every indiscretion, every sin, every lust. He's come to bring comfort in the midst of every breakup, every disinterested person you've liked, every prayer you offer that He would deliver you from what seems to be an enduring loneliness.

When you know you've messed up yet again, when you are frustrated with yourself beyond belief, when you feel ashamed and dirty, when you beat yourself up over the vicious cycle of sinning and repentance in which you live, receive the Lord's forgiveness, and then remind yourself that this is, in fact, no vicious cycle at all. You sinned. The Lord forgave you. He makes all things new. So there is no cycle. You're not going in circles or treading water. You are starting fresh every morning, renewed by His good and gracious forgiveness. Just as He is there for you, working all things for good on your behalf, so also His Gospel frees you to His good and perfect will for your life. Suddenly, things aren't looking so bad after all.

> Your Lord has something better in store for you.

One of the biggest challenges in being a Christian single is being chaste. Chastity goes beyond celibacy but includes what you look at and what you think about. One of the hardest things in the struggle to be chaste is a lack of accountability. In a marriage, the couple is still called to be chaste within their marriage (but not celibate). Yet they have each other and help each other in the Christian's struggle for chastity. In a marriage, it's much harder to do things secretively, since they are together so much of the time; whereas a single person is alone, so he can get away with things and no one else would ever know about it. A Christian single has to hold himself accountable and doesn't have another person as a part of his life to aid him in the Christian's struggle against sin.
—Ryan, mid-twenties

AND WHILE YOU'RE AT IT, DON'T MOVE IN TOGETHER EITHER

For real.

First of all, our Lord says not to. "Let marriage be held in honor among all, and let the marriage bed be undefiled" (Hebrews 13:4). So there's that, which in and of itself ought to be more than enough to keep us from wanting to set up house—sans wedding vows—with our significant others. But it's easy for us to fall into disbelief, to doubt our Lord's Word when He says not to do something. We don't really believe that our Lord means what He says. We can do exactly that which He says not to do and still get away with it, right? We don't actually buy the fact that "the wages of sin is death" (Romans 6:23). Death. That's sobering. It should stop us in our tracks when the thought of sexual impurity even dashes through our minds. That's how serious this is, how important this is to our Lord. (And, we pray, how important it is to us too.)

That's because we're sinners, and sinners don't like obeying the Ten Commandments, especially the first one, the one that warns us against having or believing in other gods. In short, it warns us against unbelief or disbelief. But when we believe that we can get away with something God has told us not to do, or when we don't think He actually means what He says, that's exactly what we're doing: not believing.

That needs to stop.

Don't Even Go There

Before you start to tell me that your boyfriend or fiancé is different than most men, or that the rent is too high and that moving in together is really just your way of being good stewards, or that you need some time to figure out if she's compatible before you dive into marriage, stop. Because that's baloney, and everyone—from your pastor to your parents—knows it. You're not fooling anybody. Not even me, and I don't even know you.

Maybe your guy is different than most men, but if he is different, let him be different in the fact that he is *not* willing to move in with you before you get married. If he is a strong man of God, if he values and cherishes you, if he listens to you and asks you questions, if he is patient and not selfish, if the only thing more important to him than you is the faith given and received in God's gifts of His Word and body and blood, if he is that kind of man, then he is different enough to be worth marrying, not worth just moving in with.

If she is different than other women, let her be different in the fact that she would never pressure you to move in together. If she is a caring woman of faith, if she hears your frustrations each day and does her best to calm them, if she is sensitive and not self-centered, if the only hope she points you to is in Christ—your Savior from all your screw-ups and unkind words—if she is that kind of woman, then she is different enough to be worth marrying. And you better not let her get away.

If the cynic in you is pooh-poohing all this; if, in your head, you're thinking, "That's a nice dream, honey. You just keep telling yourself they still make men and women like that," be assured that they do. They may be difficult to find. It may take years. But they do exist, and they are deserving of the kind of respect that our Lord gives in His Word: "Let marriage be held in honor." The men and women are worth that. They are valued and honored in God's sight, so much so that the way in which He loved them was to send His Son to die the death of Romans 6:23 (see also John 3:16–17). And if they are that important to Him, they can at least be a fraction of that worth to you.

If you're not already engaged, moving into his apartment isn't going to get you a ring. In fact, it's actually going to move the ring even farther out of your line of sight. (And he won't get you a bigger diamond to make up for it either.) Part of the urgency and the joy a man experiences in picking out a ring and proposing to the woman he loves is based in the fact that one day, after the wedding and the reception are over, he'll get to take this woman home. He'll never have to say good-bye again. He'll get to come home to her every day, eat dinner with her, hug her, and love her, forever. Anticipating that is a huge incentive; it's enough to scoot a man right along to the mall parking lot and into the jewelry store.

But when the woman is already home, when he doesn't have to say good-bye, well, suddenly the thousand dollars he's saved is look-ing like a good start to buying that flat screen he's always wanted. That's what happens when marriage isn't held in honor.

Oh, and if you're paying a lot in rent and so is she, here's an idea: you can each move to a cheaper place! Or you can get married and then move in together in a way that delights the Lord and brings Him joy. (Imagine that! You, a teacher or a construction worker or an IT consultant, gladden the heart of your Savior.) But you can't use money as an excuse to thwart the Bible. No one's buying it.

Just Do It

If, God forbid, Scripture isn't enough to convince you that co-habitation is unhelpful and unhealthy, maybe plain reason will help. It all comes down to this: cohabitation is the easy way out. It's the lazy way of having a relationship. It doesn't require commitment or effort. At the most, it takes a moving truck. At the least, it takes schlepping a bag of stuff over each week throughout the course of a couple months and then, one day, simply not leaving.

Statistically, a cohabiting couple is doomed to fail. On average, you'll get a year or two out of the relationships. If you're a woman, less than half of you will get a ring on your finger within the next three years. If you're a white woman, you have an average of nine-teen months before the relationship takes a nose dive.[9] Nineteen months! Beyond that, the latest report on the subject explains that after five years of living together outside of marriage, only 13 percent of cohabiting couples were still together. Just 13 percent. Do a little math, and discover that 87 percent of cohabiting relationships fail. They dissolve. They break up. Marriages end too; no one is disputing that. But in a cohabiting relationship, you are, even according to statistics, set up to fail. What kind of way is that to start a relationship? No way at all.

Need cheaper rent? It's just money. Want time to determine if you're right for each other? Great! Keep on dating each other. But don't move in together outside of marriage. Your Lord has something better in store for you. You can take that to the bank.

On the other hand, if you and your girlfriend are madly in love, if she is a woman who rejoices in Christ, if she will make a sterling mother and a devoted spouse, if she wants to take care of you and that makes you want to take care of her, if she respects you and listens to you, and if you are insanely and crazily attracted to her, get married. This is different—please note—than getting engaged and then waiting for fifteen years so that you can make sure the flowers are the right shade of purple or so that her second cousin thrice removed can fly in from Santa Barbara for the event. Just get married.

While marriage is more than just a place to relieve all of your sexual desires (1 Corinthians 6:13–20; 7:1–8), it is also, Paul tells us, "better to marry than to burn with passion" (1 Corinthians 7:9). Waiting around invites temptation, and Satan's already the ultimate party crasher. If the Lord has placed the right woman in your life and you are prepared to be a suitable husband; if you both understand the role of men and women and their place within the Church and their relationship with one another; if your families have given their blessing and your pastor is scheduling premarital counseling sessions; and if you are all sorts of frustrated about your singleness (let the reader understand), marry. Don't hang out for five years. Marry, be fruitful, multiply. As you do, revel in the gifts of a Father who loves you, even to the point of designing something that moves you closer to your spouse, is cause for mutual joy, and—if He wills it—provides the gift of children.

All of which is to say: Why haven't you set a date already?!

There's No Place like Home—
Except for When There Is

Families struggle with what to do with singles during big events such as holidays and family reunions and funerals. So let's talk quickly about how you as pastors and parents and siblings and crazy uncles can care for the single people in your midst when they are most in need of it.

Don't tell me! I already know: you're sick of hearing about single people. Well, strangely enough, they're sick of hearing about you married people. They're sick of your Instagram pictures of heart-shaped foam in your coffee on Valentine's Day and your Facebook album of cutting down your Christmas tree with your husband at Christmas and how you had someone to hold your hand at Grandma's funeral.

It doesn't mean they're right. They're just tired of hearing about it. They're tired of hearing about how you have what they want. During these sorts of life-changing moments, every feeling they have about being single is growing like a well-watered Chia Pet.

That's why I'm proposing that instead of us all being sick of one another, we take care of one another. Families, invite the single people over for Thanksgiving. Single people, go. Families, don't invite them to the event where there are forty-seven other couples there. It's intimidating and the singles won't go. Single people, get tough. You'll get through this.

Families, meet them on middle ground outside of weddings and funerals and all the times you *have* to get together. Instead of having them over for supper, where they're going to feel like they're being interrogated under bright lights by the CIA, ask to meet them at a coffee shop where everyone's on unfamiliar ground. Singles, you have time for coffee. Just do it. Families, if you do invite singles over, ask them if they want to bring a friend. Singles, they're being nice. Don't hole up at home.

Take care of one another already, okay? You know you can do that.

One final thing: Singles, when these big occasions loom in your future, you're going to feel a lot better about the suffering you are enduring if you do three things: (1) Pray. The Lord answers prayers. He hears them. Don't pretend to be a valiant martyr. Tell Him you are alone and that it stinks and that you're totally over being single and that if you have to be the seventeenth wheel at one more family Christmas, you are going to blow a gasket. He will understand. (2) Love. Take care of the families around you. Instead of waiting for someone to ask you over for Labor Day, invite people over yourself. There is great joy to be had in taking care of those the Lord has placed in your life. (3) Toughen up. Being alone in these kinds of circumstances isn't a pleasure trip, but the Lord will see you through. You can be resilient. You can choose not to spend your entire Easter break snapping at your mom and bemoaning the fact that no one in your family understands you. Because they do, and they are sorry you are hurting. So, straighten up, little soldier. It's going to be a wild ride.

Chapter 9

Awkward Breakups
and Other Things Singles Could
Definitely, Totally Do Without

He was tall and handsome, smart and quick. We were both students at the same school, both studying, both hard workers. It only took a date—a dinner and a play—for me to be smitten. He was the one. The era of awkward first dates was over.

We spent our first summer apart. He was living in Rome, studying Latin, and I was in Indiana, studying every line of every e-mail he sent my way. It was a romantic summer, filled with promises of European travel, flowers delivered to my door while we were video chatting together, and dreams of eating gelato in front of the Trevi Fountain. Elizabeth Bennett and Mr. Darcy had nothing on me.

It was, consequently, the same summer that warning flares started exploding all over the place, blowing up in my face right and left like a fireworks display gone awry. Like any good female, I doused them with water, pretended they didn't exist, and tried harder than ever to prove to him that I was the girl for him.

It didn't work. After a year together, of premarital counseling sessions, arguments, sleepless nights, and more confusion than I experience trying to drive my way out of a roundabout, he called the engagement off, in my office, over lunch.

My family, best friend, and pastor were a cocoon of comfort. My sisters made sure I ate, even when I could hardly choke down my favorite foods. My little nephew hugged me every time he saw tears forming in my eyes, even though he was too young to understand why I was crying. My best friend drove four hours to sit with me while I stared out the window in shock. My pastor called every day, reminding me that I was prayed for and that the single Christian has freedom in whom she marries, that if this marriage were not God's will, it was not the end for me. My parents got in the car the moment they heard and started driving my way.

A few days later, my ex-fiancé was back: penitent, ashamed, and quiet. He bought flowers and an unnecessarily expensive dinner and asked, with his head hanging low, if I would take his ring back. I did, figuring this was God's answer to my screams and wails and tears and prayers over the past three days. Forgiveness came quickly and readily, and for twenty-four blissful hours, everything was as it should be.

Until he changed his mind. Again. This time, he was sure. He *really* didn't want to get married. He didn't want me to have his children. And in his parting words, he told me that if he had his choice, he'd rather be alone than with me. He didn't need to say any more. That one cut deeply, and I showed him the door while biting my lip so hard I thought it would bleed.

I spent days, weeks—actually, well into two years—sobbing over the relationship, the marriage, that never was. I lost weight, cried in the aisles of Target for no reason, heard people talking about the two of us when I passed them in hallways, and suffered the greatest embarrassment I had known yet in life. I felt panicked, desperate to move out of my apartment where that last, awful conversation took place, while simultaneously frantic to stay in the same place on the off chance that one day he would change his mind and need to find me. (That desperate feeling, I imagine, is what life is like apart from Christ. It is fundamentally shifting, never solid. It's hopeless. It's suffocating, leaving you depressed and exhausted.)

However, there were hopeful moments in those dark days. My family and my church family all cared for and about me in unique and profound ways. My sisters continued to make me laugh. My parents prayed for me and doused me with more love than I deserved. My pastor assured me, as only he could, that Christ would love me despite even this. My friends offered to chase a certain gentleman down with shotguns and shovels and came up with hilarious and unconventional ways to get me to leave my apartment.

Even my teachers looked out for me. One day, I passed a professor on the sidewalk. As we got closer to one another, he yelled, "Stop!" I froze. He stared at me intently for a moment and then nodded to himself. "You're okay," he confirmed and kept on walking. I didn't know what he meant at first, but then I realized that this pastor, using his years of experience caring for his parishioners in the congregation, knew that I was going to be all right. His diagnosis was a relief, enough to let me know that he was concerned and available to talk and that I would survive.

Like a long roll of bubble wrap, each of these brothers and sisters in the faith rolled me up in everything that was good and perfect for me, protecting me from what was the harshest reality I had, to that point, experienced. And for that—for their Christian care and prayer—I will always be grateful. It's easy to give to others; it's harder to receive. When people are concerned for you, even if you don't want them to be, you let them care for you because it's as important to them as it is to you. When one member of the Body of Christ suffers, we all do.

"Heaven has no rage like love to hatred turned," wrote William Congreve, "Nor hell a fury like a woman scorned."[1] I eventually grew to be angry over what had happened and the words that were spoken, to be sure, but I was hurt too, a broken, hot mess with a side of a drama. I vacillated between sobbing in the shower to putting on a brave face at work to feeling numb sitting in the pew at church. I told people who inquired, "Oh, I'm fine," putting on the bravest of fronts to prove I was tough, that I could handle it.

But as soon as I locked my apartment door behind me, I cried at everything, at turning off the lights and being in the dark at night, of having to see people who were his friends, at seeing his name pop up in my Facebook news feed. I skipped the wedding of a dear friend that year, something I still regret, unable to handle the thought of watching a wedding taking place only weeks before mine was supposed to have been. I was irritated too, downright mad, at those who said, in an effort to comfort me, that I'd find someone else or that it was better that it happened now.

Those experiences made everything more awful. It felt like the only thing worse than getting dumped was getting asked about and prayed over because I was dumped. One of my classmates caught me studying in the library one afternoon. "I didn't know you were getting married!" she squealed. "I'm not," I replied, fully aware I was being awfully rude while moving purposefully toward the door.

"Oh, my gosh!" she exclaimed. "Can I ask what happened?" I sighed and stopped. By now, I was pretty good at giving my fifteen-second recap spiel. He fundamentally rejects what I stand for as a person. He thinks I don't communicate. He doesn't want me to have his children. Whatever. Pick your poison. Engaged. Unengaged. Engaged. Unengaged. So. Totally. Unengaged. I was hopeful that was enough, that she'd say she was sorry and then move on. It didn't work.

"Can you come here for a minute?" she asked, pointing to the library conference room. I followed her, figuring she had a similar story to tell. Instead, she shut the door behind us, grabbed my hands, closed her eyes, and started praying. She prayed for me, and for him, and for him and me, and for me and him, and for engaged couples everywhere, and for unengaged singles everywhere, and for people who are married, and people who aren't married, and people who might someday consider getting married, and people who like being married, and people whom marriage doesn't seem to like, and then, just when my eyes couldn't get any wider, she started crying.

Suddenly, it was about her suffering and not about mine, which is not a bad thing. But it somehow made everything worse. I longed for the prayers of others, but not the kind that involved being dragged into dark library corners with too few tissues. It was too much. It was time to move on.

Two years, a new job, and a move to a different city later, I was still struggling, anxious to find my identity on my own, without him, but unsure of how to do it. Visits with a counselor, prayer that sometimes morphed into bitter words of anger, and time all did their paced and deliberate work. Slowly, almost imperceptibly, eventually, the pain started to lessen. I thought of him more infrequently, cried

> The Lord molded and shaped me, pruned and formed me for life under the cross.

less, began to remember what life without another person was like.

Like an icicle melting in the spring, he and his memory simply melted down and faded away. I'm not sure when it happened. I don't know that I even realized it. But I do know that one day I thought of him and realized I couldn't remember the last time I had. That was the day I felt like Adriane again. Just Adriane. Single Adriane. But the Adriane that was still standing, still breathing, still here, by the grace of God.

The marriage that wasn't no longer causes me pain or angst. He is simply another way in which the Lord molded and shaped me, pruned and formed me for life under the cross, life according to His perfect plan and will. I'm not the only one who has known suffering as the result of a broken relationship.

Things You Probably Should Never Say

The more people learned about what had happened, the more they stepped forward to share with me their own stories of loss. And the more I listened, the more I recognized all we had in common. The biggest one? We all knew exactly what we *didn't* want to hear.

"Just as soon as you quit looking, you'll find someone."

I hate that phrase. I heard it a million times in the years following my broken, messed-up engagement. What I wanted to say, each and every time someone glibly tossed that little nugget out was, "I've quit. Trust me. I'm not looking. I'm *so* not looking. I'm so not looking I'm blindfolded. I've plucked my eyes out. I don't even have eyeballs! Now what are you going to do?"

Advice-givers are well-intentioned. They mean to give us some kind of hope, that there is still a chance we'll meet someone, still the potential for a happily ever after. What they fail to recognize is that their comments sting. Some of us have almost completely given up. We're actually a little hopeless and maybe even mostly despondent at this point. If ever there were a group of people not looking, it's us.

Still, the Lord has chosen not to bless us with a spouse.

That means one of two things: Either (1) the Lord's gift of a spouse has nothing to do with us looking or not looking, or (2) see number 1.

That's the problem with this statement: It puts the onus on us. It pretends that there's something we can do to change or alter the course God has set for our lives. It makes us believe that finding a person to love, honor, and cherish is a work we can accomplish. It brings us shame, as though we're doing something wrong. It hurts, because it seems we aren't doing enough. It is a painful reminder that once again, we are different—isolated and alone.

The gifts our Lord has to give aren't dependent on how hard we work or don't, if we're still looking or if we've quit, if we've been engaged three times or never at all. Gifts are just that. They're given, not earned. They have much to say about the giver, and not just the receiver.

Indeed, a spouse is truly a gift. It's not something promised in Scripture. God never promises to bless us with a spouse or with children. He doesn't guarantee us a whirlwind romance, a fairy tale wedding, and a *Sound of Music*-esque lineup of tidy children.

What He does promise is our salvation. He promises us forgiveness of sins. He promises us that He will love us, fill all our needs, and be our rest. He promises us comfort, joy, an eternity with Him in heaven. He promises to hear our prayers and even perhaps to change His mind because of them. (We see this in Exodus, when Moses pleaded with the Lord not to destroy Israel after God got slightly miffed about that whole golden calf situation.)

So, to all of you pastors and parents and friends and random strangers off the street who feel you're in a position to make comments on our love lives even though we've actually never met, please don't make us promises that our Lord Himself isn't even willing to make. Don't tell us that finding a spouse is up to us and our behavior and our eyeballs. Don't tempt us to believe that you know God's good plan and purpose for our lives better than He does.

Instead, bear with us. Listen to us be frustrated. Hand over a tissue when we are grieving that which we want but aren't given. Tell us you're sorry that it hurts. Explain to us that you understand how difficult it can be to be lonely. Remind us of the one who suffered all so that He could suffer this alongside us. Make us mindful of our Baptism. Help us remember that our value and worth come from Christ, not from a spouse.

In those moments, and even in the perfectly normal ones, encourage us not to fall into the temptation to be like Rachel, who "refuses to be comforted" (Jeremiah 31:15). It is easy for us to step into the trap of feeling sorry for ourselves. We think that no one understands us because of the cross we bear. But you, our friends and families, our pastors and congregations, our co-workers and bosses, you do understand.

"Maybe you've already forgotten how much more stress we single ladies live with," a friend once texted me following my engagement. The statement wounded me, even if it was offered as a half-joke, because the truth was: I hadn't forgotten. I won't forget. Defined by being single for years, shamed at essentially being dumped at the altar, being single was my identity. But I had also realized, years ago in my singleness, that I had a choice: I could choose to be Eeyore, perpetually down, gloomy, frustrated, and annoyed. Or I could acknowledge my cross—suffering in the dark moments and rejoicing in the bright ones—while remaining thankful to God for all the gifts He *has* chosen to give.

One of my professors from the seminary did exactly what all singles need: He was honest with me. Following my broken engagement, he wouldn't simply say, "Jesus loves you" as he dashed past me. Instead, he acknowledged what was true: "No matter what people say, it's not going to fix anything now," and "Don't worry; with the recession, he'll totally lose money on the ring," and other equally helpful sentiments. He didn't pity me or let me feel awful. He was candid.

Fellow Christians, don't let us wallow, but don't try to tell us that being single isn't difficult. It is, and it's more thorny when we're given false hope. Please, if you care about us at all, don't tell us that if we quit looking, the Lord will drop the man or woman of our dreams into our laps because we're not looking. He hasn't promised that. Just tell us instead that we're baptized, we're forgiven, we're loved, and we're normal.

And guess what?

That will be enough.

"So I know this girl . . ."

I take that back. Tell us about your friends. Tell us why they're so awesome and would make great spouses. We need to hear that there are good single people who still exist in the world. It gives us hope. Tomorrow looks a little brighter when we hear that we're not alone. And as long as you're telling us about your single friends, set us up with them. It's okay. But do it sparingly. And please, for the love of all that's good, don't assume that just because two people are breathing means that they should get married. There's a tendency in Christian circles for a well-intentioned person to think, "Well, Peter has a pulse. And he's nice. And Sarah has a pulse. And she's nice. They should be together!"

Contrary to popular belief, we're more than just our ability to breathe. We're more than our personalities. In fact, we have thoughts and opinions. We have books we like and movies we don't. Some of us love funky kinds of foods, and others won't think beyond tuna sandwiches. Some of us are very particular about our need for naps, and some of us can survive on four hours of sleep a night. That is to say, our Lord has created us with unique quirks that make us wonderfully odd to some people and delightfully attractive to others. He's given us particular needs and interests, desires and thoughts, and those aren't things that ought to be set aside simply to entice a member of the opposite sex.

Let us be us. Let us be the people God has created us to be. It's better that way. Trust us.

If you happen to have a friend, or a brother, or a co-worker, or a pastor who is single, who shares at least a few of our interests, and who has been praying for a holy and pious relationship, then tell us all about him. Tell us why you think we'd be edifying to each other, what it is about us that will serve and benefit the other person. Because if you do that, if you take time and care in the people you introduce us to, and if you don't just throw people at us for the sake of trying to marry us off, we may both just find that this dating thing isn't quite as awful as we thought.

Maybe.

"You dodged a bullet with that last one."

No, really? You think we don't know that our last relationship ended horribly, that we are ashamed and embarrassed of failing—yet again—at finding the kind of love our friends and parents have? Trust us: There are moments, when we are sitting at home on Friday night creating fake wedding boards on Pinterest or watching the fourth basketball game of the day, where we realize, quite clearly, that we've been either (a) drunk, (b) drugged, (c) asleep, or (d) desperate when it comes to the people we pick to date.

It's harder to recognize it in the moment, when we've finally found ourselves a person who actually wants to spend time with us, that that person isn't the right one, and hindsight—that darn teacher in 20/20—is one of the few ways we recognize it. Women, especially, are great at sticking around in awful relationships for months, years, decades even. We convince ourselves that it's really not all that bad, that if we change just a little, try harder, act a different way, cut our hair, learn to cook better, or ask fewer questions, the men in our lives will show us the love we crave.

It very rarely works. Often, we are left heartbroken. Alone, we are unsure of who we are and struggle to find our identity apart from the person who's just broken our heart or whose heart we've just broken. And then, when a well-meaning friend or aunt or co-worker gleefully comforts us in the knowledge that we've "dodged a bullet," as though that's somehow supposed to make us feel good about what's happened, it not only reopens the wound but it also slices a brand new one. There is hurt that we've not yet found "the one," to be sure; even more, we are hurt that we are again alone. In our suffering, we become like the children of Israel wandering in the desert, convinced that we are better enslaved back in Egypt, miserable, but at least warm and well fed. We fail to see that the Lord has something else in mind. We want what's not ours, what we can't have. In that moment, we'd rather be hurting with our ex than hurting alone.

So rather than letting out a huge "Whooee!" followed by an expletive and a "You sure did dodge a bullet on that crazy chick, bro!" please just tell us you're sorry. Let us know that it grieves you to see us hurt. Ask what you can pray for with regard to our broken, severed relationship. Acknowledge that we are hurting. Remind us that time is our friend and that in a few months (or maybe years), it won't hurt as badly as it does now.

You may be right; we probably did dodge a bullet. But the point in time that you want to tell us that is probably the exact point in time that we don't (or can't) hear it. Instead, hug us, reassure us, and tell us to get ourselves to church. We may not thank you for it, but we'll know in our hearts that you're right.

"Well, if I were you..."

Hey, guess what? You're not us.

That would be a punchy way to end the conversation but maybe not the most helpful. In this statement, we see one of our worst habits: to offer advice that isn't asked for. We use it as a filler, an easy way to fill space when we don't know what to say or do next. And let's get real: We love to talk about ourselves. We're selfish that way.

Singles don't need to hear yet another story about how you met your wife on a flight to Miami (because we fly all the time and that's never happened to us), what you did when your crazy ex showed up at your wedding completely trashed (well, that was awkward), and which bar has the cutest bartender working during happy hour (not really our scene).

> The Lord has our future—even our present—under complete control.

Stories now and then can give us hope. But when we pour our hearts out to you about the pain we feel and the longing we experience, your own drama isn't what we need. We just need you to listen. We need you to understand and nod your head. We need you to acknowledge that we're hurting. We need to know someone understands all the confusion and angst.

You don't have to fix us. You just have to listen.

"I don't understand why you're not married!"

Acceptable response: "Well, sweetheart, that makes two of us." Not acceptable response: "I don't get it either! I mean, I *do* only have nine toes, and I've read online it's not cool to be still sleeping with a Cabbage Patch at age 32, but, really, I have an *amazing* personality, I promise you!"

Actually, this one works. One of my friends once told me, "The fact that you're still single is more mysterious than the Lord's Supper." It was the most theologically kind and random statement he could have made. It acknowledged my pain and confusion. It gave voice to the fact that the Lord's will doesn't always make sense, even if it is perfect. It was a compliment in a weirdly humorous sort of way.

Whether we are married or single, we would do well to affirm our friends in this: that "My [God's] thoughts are not your thoughts, neither are your ways My ways" (Isaiah 55:8). Our tendency as sinners is to assume that we know what is best for ourselves, but we never bother to consider that He who created the very universe might have something different in mind for us. It doesn't mean that it makes sense to us; our Lord's words don't provide us with a bulleted list of why we're not working on seating charts and picking tuxes. But it does confirm what we knew: that the Lord has our future—even our present—under complete control. And that's coming through loud and clear!

HEY, MARRIED PEOPLE, ACT LIKE YOU LIKE IT ALREADY!

Nothing is more of a bummer to a single person than to hear a husband or a wife say sarcastically, "Well, I hope you're living up your single days now, because, boy, when you get married, the fun is sure over!"

Married couples, stop that nonsense. Single people, consider the two following options as responses: (1) "I'm going to punch you in the nose." (Then proceed to punch said person in the nose.) Or (2) "I'm really sad to hear that. The Lord's gift of marriage is one of His best, and it's hard to hear you don't see it that way. So, now I'm going to punch you in the nose."

One of the worst possible ways to attempt to make a single person feel better about not being married is to degrade and diminish the value of marriage. Marriage is a blessing, a union designed by God in which men and women are given "an all-encompassing sharing of life," as Dr. Robert George, McCormick Professor of Jurisprudence at Princeton University and Chair of the United States Commission on International

Religious Freedom, told a gathering of Lutherans in August 2013. "Like other bonds—friendship between siblings, parents and children—marriage involves a union of hearts and minds. But in the case of marriage, its all-encompassingness refers to its distinctive feature, that is, in addition to being a union of hearts and minds, it's a bodily union, where the bodily union is made possible and intelligible by the sexual reproductive complimentary-ness of man and woman." It's a union that is "pledged to permanence," he told us, and along with that, to sexual fidelity.

Those who are married no doubt find it easy to take this for granted. (That's what we sinners do when the Lord gives us a good thing.) And while they are busy being frustrated that their wives routinely turns their white T-shirts pink in the wash while their husbands have a strange inability to get the trash from the kitchen to the dumpster, their single friends are watching in abject horror.

"That's what I want!" singles are virtually screaming. "I want to share my life completely and wholly with my spouse. I want to be joined to my husband (or wife) mentally and emotionally. I want to know him physically too, and I don't just mean sex. I want to be assured that he will hug and love and hold me permanently—forever!—and that he'll be faithful and true, even when I'm driving him nuts. I want that!" (If you watch closely, you may just notice that when we're done throwing that brief tantrum, we do even, on occasion, stamp our foot. Hey, if it works for your three-year-old, it works for us.)

Telling us that marriage stinks doesn't make us not desire it. We would rather be joined with a strong man or woman of God and suffer alongside him or her than to continue to suffer alone. Tell us marriage is difficult and that it has its challenges. Make it clear that dating or getting engaged or being married doesn't make all our problems go away, but that it does give us the opportunity and the joy to slog through them alongside someone else. Remind us that suffering is evident in everyone's lives (hey, thanks, Adam and Eve), but that it can and will look different for married couples than for those who are single.

And then stop talking (seriously, you should have this part figured out by now) and listen to us. Let us share with you our concerns and our fears about what relationships and marriage may look like. Then, when we've spilled our guts and you're left to clean up the mess, point us in the direction of Jesus and give us a gentle nudge. He is the one who draws us to Himself, who cares for the lonely and the ones who need space, who loves the single and the married, who chooses suffering unique to the widow and the wife. And He does it all well.

Chapter 10

The Danger of Fantasy

Winston Churchill talked about enigmas wrapped in riddles inside of mysteries. He might well have been talking about relationships. Or the female mind because, let's face it, it's virtually impossible to understand *that*. Or he might have been talking about what it means to be a Christian single. Or how they get those jalapeños in those little tiny holes in olives.

One of those enigmas is the way in which men and women struggle in an unhelpful tension between fantasy and reality. Fantasy is fun. Reality is hard work. The culture encourages fantasy. It thumbs its nose at reality. Fantasy is mysterious. Reality is obvious. Both are dangerous. Both cause heartbreak. Both can cause singles to despair and to doubt. Fantasy makes it easy to build up the opposite sex in our minds, to create ideas and expectations of what relationships ought to look like. That can be fun, and it's certainly easy. But we forget, as we begin to live those expectations out or to act on them or to expect them, that they are quite often very different than reality. And not in good ways. In fact, they're not even vaguely reminiscent of it.

Women love fantasies because women love emotion. Maybe it's romantic comedies. Maybe it's the Marlboro Man's chaps and biceps. Maybe it's "I know he's treated me awfully before, but this time it'll be different." Maybe it's "Getting married will fix all my problems." Men love fantasies because they thrive on the visual. Perhaps they choose pornography as their fantasy du jour. Well, not "perhaps." Statistics prove they actually do. "With annual revenues exceeding $13 billion in the United States and $97 billion worldwide, the porn industry is bigger than Microsoft, Google, Amazon, eBay, Yahoo!, Apple, Netflix, and EarthLink *combined*."[1]

Perhaps we should stop for just a moment to talk about pornography, whether it's looked at by men or women. Porn is the perfect fantasy because it can be acted on in private. It's isolated. It's solitary. Men and women can be alone with their fantasies, and they force reality to flee for a time.

But it's also the worst fantasy. The devil, using his wiliest tactics, reels people in. "Who will know?" he says innocently. "Did God really say you couldn't look at porn? Will there really be any downside if you do take a peek?"

And peek they do. Again and again and again. "In a 2004 U.S. Senate hearing, Dr. Mary Anne Layden, of the University of Pennsylvania's Department of Psychiatry, testified that the brain scans of adults viewing pornography were similar to those of cocaine users."[2]

That's how the devil thwarts reality. He draws men into their fantasies, encourages them to indulge in it, and hooks them on it like a drug addict who can't go a day without getting a fix. But then comes the fantasy's greatest irony: it shames you. You're embarrassed. The feeling of condemnation is overwhelming. "You did *what?*" the devil gasps in horror. "How could you do something so awful? How could you look at those pictures or watch that movie? Some Christian you are!"

That's why fantasies don't work. The devil, the world, and our sinful nature tempt us to sin and then taunt us unceasingly when we give in. It's the worst of vicious cycles, a never-ending circle of "What can it hurt?" and "You've hurt everyone and everything around you!" No matter the fantasy, when reality hits, things get broken. Whether it's Ryan Gosling's "Hey, girl" memes or the latest issue of *Playboy*, fantasies don't work. Ever. They are dangerous. They cut deeply. They are addicting. They isolate you.

Beware of that which is not reality. Stay firmly rooted in right here, right now. Our Lord is here at work for you in this place, in this moment. He has a plan for you, even though it may not feel like it. He has only good gifts for you, even when it doesn't seem like it. He doesn't want you to live in a fake world; He wants you to live in the world He created, in what's tangible, what's earthy.

Reality is hard, but fantasies can be dangerous. So, "resist the devil, and he will flee from you" (James 4:7). With the Lord's help, fight that bugger. And fight him out loud! Don't just fight him in your head. Say the Lord's Prayer out loud. Make the sign of the cross. Get out your hymnal and sing, "Satan, hear this proclamation: I am baptized into Christ!"[3] Because he will hear, and he will listen, and he will flee. The Lord will see to that.

Getting back to reality: There's a temptation for singles to fall off one side of the horse or the other. (Unless, of course, you don't ride horses, in which case, [1] what's wrong with you? and [2] boy, that analogy *bombed*.) Singles either believe ourselves to be martyrs, solemn but resilient, ready to face our fate like Joan of Arc in chain mail, or we believe we are warriors, claiming to love our independence and even, on occasion, bellowing out with a Mel Gibson/William Wallace-esque bravado, "*Freedom!*" (This is generally the point at which our horse stumbles, our kilts blow in the wind, and we are left defenseless on the ground with no shield and no hope. The Lord does have a certain way of keeping us humble.)

However, like country music has told us, we're all white liars. There is actually nothing particularly noble about being single, nor is being single a mark of history-making courage. We don't gain anyone's respect by moping around in our pajamas, Instagramming pictures of empty ice cream cartons, and wearing our hair in messy ponytails because we don't have the energy to shower. Likewise, we don't do ourselves any favors by blowing off the opposite sex, by pretending we are too important to be bothered with their existence, by tweeting, "Men: can't live with them, can't shoot them."

This sets up a false reality. It tells the world that waiting for what the Lord has in store for you is either tantamount to listening to Taylor Swift on repeat (that's the martyr part, for those of you who were unsure) or that it's a drain on your existence to have to deal with people and all their, you know, breathing.

What We Do Know

Here is what we do know: Being single is difficult, whether you think it's the end of the world or whether you love the idea of your independence. But it is also a balance. Some days you'll feel as though you are suffering beyond what you can handle, that your house is like a monastery and that you are, in general, misunderstood. Some days you will rejoice that you come home to an empty house, to popcorn for supper and the ability to sleep sideways in bed.

Being single is a balance. Those feelings are normal. You're not crazy. Other people feel the same way you do. (They may be crazy, but you're not. At least, that's what I want you to tell yourself.) Being single, for all its difficulty, is also the Lord's plan for you right now. It may not be tomorrow. It may be for the next six years. You don't know. Only He does. But you are His, and He has redeemed you. You are baptized, declared righteous for the sake of Jesus, another single.

He knows your martyr complex. He hears your war cry of awesomeness. You don't scare Him. He's not freaked out by you. He loves you. He comforts you. He gives you peace, a peace that is so full and perfect and yours that it surpasses your own capacity to understand it.

So, ride the horse steady in the saddle. Pray that the Lord would keep you from both sides. Rejoice that He plants you firmly in the middle. And when you fall out of it, when you find yourself dumped onto a gravel road watching the horse's tail feathers—wait, wrong animal, I mean, rump? hindquarters?

Take 2.

When you find yourself watching your horse gallop off into the sunset, take heart. This world is Christ's. He will not allow you to know pain or grief beyond what you can handle. Your future has already been determined, and it has been set in place by the one who has washed away all your mopey and dramatic tendencies in the waters of Holy Baptism.

You are not a martyr. You are not a warrior. You are a child loved by God, and that's enough.

This chapter brought to you by the time I fell off a horse and slid down a gravel road wearing jean shorts. That's another life lesson for Book 2.

Three Easy Steps to Complete Happiness (Or Its Lesser Title: "Psyche! We Were Just Playing")

You know better than that. There's no magic formula, no scientific logarithm that can change your longing for a spouse or fix the way in which you understand what it is you're supposed to be doing as a single. The good news? There are a lot of things you can be doing that you're probably already doing! Like praying. (Bet you didn't see that one coming, did you?) Pray for what you want. Don't hold back. If you want to marry the hot guy who sits two pews ahead of you in church but has never given you a second glance, pray for it. If you desire a wife and a household full of well-cared-for little baptized Christian babies, pray for it. Do that. Pray, even if it feels like the guy doesn't notice or the Lord isn't hearing you.

Prayer is one of your Father's kindest and most tender gifts to you. He doesn't cut you off or keep you out of the loop. He draws you in and invites your thoughts. He wants to know what scares you, what keeps you awake at night, what you wonder about, what are the desires of your heart.

Keep praying. Our Lord delights to hear what you long for, even those things that seem mundane and boring and dull. Tell Him what you want in a spouse. Tell Him you're lonely. Tell Him you desire to learn to be the man who gives or the woman who receives. Tell Him you're perfectly content. Tell Him you just want to understand.

Just talk. He will listen, and He will answer.

You can also consider Scripture, which tells us to be content with what we have. This is nearly impossible. (I personally think it's unachievable.) But it's worth trying. So while you're single, make good use of the time. Be the best aunt you can be. Be a killer cousin. Pick up the slack at church. If your co-worker needs someone to take a shift so that he can get to parent-teacher conferences, step in. Prove that you're committed to whatever vocation the Lord has put you in right now: whether you're studying to be a surgeon or a landscaper or you're a wannabe stay-at-home mother. Show the world that being single doesn't have to hold you back from life one bit.

That doesn't, on the other hand, mean that you have to pretend everything is okay. If you don't want to be single, if sitting at home alone on New Year's Eve is not your idea of a good time, if it feels like everyone else has had a boyfriend or girlfriend except for you, be honest. (One of my ex-boyfriends dumped me just days before Christmas for a girl he'd been seeing on the side [Or was I the one on the side? I was never really clear on that point], so I'm not going to pretend that I loved being huddled up in sweatpants, going through four boxes of tissues over a holiday weekend.) But I will tell you that you will survive, that being single isn't the end of the world, that the Lord has good work for you to do in this period of your life.

If you are dating someone, think back to what we learned about what it means to be a man, a giver, and what it means to be a woman, a receiver. Does your relationship mirror that? Talk to your boy or girl about it. Pray about it. Does that person confess the same faith that you do? If not, is he or she willing to learn, to speak with your pastor, to go to catechesis? Start patterning the relationship of Christ and His Church now. Go to church together. Do devotions together. My husband read Scripture and prayed with me using the *Treasury of Daily Prayer* over the phone every night. Start now.

It won't seem like it at first, but people will notice. They'll notice that you're different, that you believe that what the Lord says is truest and best. You'll stand out from the crowd. You'll be set apart. And in that, you will gain respect.

That's because much of what you will encounter in the world—even people—will tend to be quick and easy, to take the simplest way out possible. But you, you have depth, you have meaning, you have worth in Christ. What's quickest and easiest and simplest isn't always what is best.

Take relationship cues from Him, from the one who created you. Don't rush into a relationship just to be in one. Take a breath. Here's why:

> *Our Lord took six whole days to make creation. He*
> *didn't hammer it out in seconds. He worked at it.*
> *He's a personal being who loves what He does, who*
> *creates art, who savors and enjoys the process as*
> *much as the product. He interacts with us. He gets*

*His hands dirty. He loves the smell of the dirt, the
way this or that feels in His hands. He loves how this
curve looks, how that angle feels. He's anything but
superficial. He takes time. He works hard. He does
nothing half-heartedly.*[4]

So it is with you and with the one that the Lord may or may not
have in store for you. Remember, if you can, that this is what your
parents and pastors and friends and this book have tried to teach
you, what they've tried to instill in you: a desire for holy and pure
relationships, a thirst to understand what it means to be a man and
what it means to be a woman, to do more digging when loneliness
and pain set in, to be deeply entrenched in the holy things of God,
not to settle, even when it seems like there is no other way out. And
in our age, that's something.

CONSIDER YOUR PARENTS. NOT EVEN KIDDING.

Plop yourselves down in your beanbag chair. Hold onto the
kitchen table. I'm about to make a radical suggestion that
will undoubtedly leave you reeling or assuming that I've
just been released from a home for the ridiculously insane.
Ready? Here it is: Talk to your parents, even if you're fifty and
they're almost dead. They aren't the backward Neanderthals
you think they are. (All right, maybe they are; they may not
get Facebook or texting or "The Interwebs.") But your parents, your family, or if not them, your pastors, really do have
your best interests at heart. They don't want you to be lonely.
They want you to find a godly wife or husband. They want
you to have a wife who makes you buffalo chicken dip just
because she knows it's your favorite. They want you to have a
husband who brings you a bouquet of flowers, not because
he's done something wrong, but simply for no reason.

Here's the other weird thing: your parents, your elders, your pastors, those older than you, are actually pretty smart. Contrary to opinion polls, they are not out to get you. They are not out to ruin your life or meddle.

Entirely.

Well, maybe just a little.

These are the people who don't just want you to be happy. They want you to do what's right, to be truthful, to be good citizens, kind friends, and, very likely in the near future, faithful husbands and wives and parents yourselves.

These are, after all, the parents who made sure you got to church every Sunday, who helped pack your lunch, who flagged the bus down when you were late for the fourth time that week (Seriously. Why were you always late in middle school?), who sat through your squeaky, shrill (let's be honest) horrible clarinet solos in junior high band, who sent money to you last month when you ran out, who listened to your incoherent rambling and sobbing when your first boyfriend broke your heart, who didn't freak out (too much) when you totally bombed a test, who rejoiced with you at your first real job, and who now simply listen to you when you hurt.

These are the parents who prayed for you, who spent hours begging our Lord to keep you safe, to help you succeed, to lead you in commendable, healthy, robust paths. And He did.

So don't be afraid to talk to your parents, to your pastor, and to people in your church who have healthy and robust marriages. Don't be afraid to let them introduce you to someone. Ask them to pray for you. Talk to them about the man or woman you pray the Lord gives you. Let them help you. They want to.

Finally, remember that there is a difference in being alone and being lonely. If you are single, you are lonely. But you are not alone. You're never alone.

The Bible says, "It's not good for man to be alone," and Scripture is right. With Christ, you aren't alone. So when you are tired, when being alone or failed relationships seem to be never-ending, when you want to give up, when you feel like you just can't go a day more, when your vision becomes blurred from frustration or anger or sadness, from fear or uncertainty, remember this: You have faithful people among you, praying for you, looking out for you. You're lonely, but you're not alone. The good and perfect plan for your life is not yours at all, but the Lord working through and by you.

That, ultimately, is the good news, the joy for those of us who are single: the Lord preserves us despite ourselves. He will provide. You will move forward, and the loneliness won't always be so difficult, because God is good.

So, if there's one thing you remember from this chapter, let it be this: only 9 percent of women and 2 percent of men say they've found a relationship at a bar or club, so you're really better off hitting up Starbucks if you want to.

No, that's not what you should remember! Remember this: these worries about being single, about finding the right man or woman, about who you will marry or if you'll ever marry at all, these are the crosses that you will suffer. But they are also the fears that will keep you close to God. Such things teach us to pray. They make us completely and wholly reliant upon His love and His mercy. They teach us that it's not up to us, that Christ is who sees us through in this world. In the midst of all these things you're feeling, all your worries, all your excitement, know this: being single is hard, but you aren't alone.

It sounds cliché, namely, because, well, it is. But there is some truth to every cliché. You really aren't alone. Our Lord has known about you and your life and this day and what you're thinking right now, about what you would major in in college, about what job you'll get or girl you'll marry or boss you'll deal with, since eternity. He is the one who is with you, the one who has a good plan and a good purpose for your life, the one alone whose promise is sure: "I will never leave you nor forsake you" (Hebrews 13:5).

Being single is hard, but don't be discouraged. Not today. You won't get your way in all things. Being single won't always be so hard. It won't always be so easy. But be patient. Be encouraged. God has a plan for you, and He will work it, and that is good enough.

Chapter 11

We Will Be Understood

*I*t *will be all right. Hold out hope. There's plenty of fish in the sea.* Now that we've given an obligatory nod to all the pat answers the world has to offer, let's consider in what we can take joy in this life, single or dating or married or widowed or divorced, until the day of the resurrection.

Cultivate an Active Prayer Life

Let's face it: You're single. You have the time. Write down the names of your friends who are single and pray for them. Pray for those of your acquaintances who are dating or engaged. Don't forget the married ones. Pray for them all!

One of the kindest text messages I've ever received was from a future pastor, still studying at the seminary. Hearing of my marriage, he texted me: "Before bed, I pray for all the brothers and sisters who have not been given someone yet. And, FYI, I was thrilled to quit praying for you in that regard." Let's be that guy. (Not *that* guy. But, you know, *this* guy.) Let's be the guys and gals who pray.

I often hear people say, "Well, prayer is good, but what can I actually *do*?" You can pray. Prayer is better than any dinner invitation, any date, any call or e-mail, anything. Prayer moves the heart of our Father. He hears us. He listens. He answers. He's promised all of that to us, and we hold Him to it.

I prayed for years that God would send me a godly husband, and then the time came that I stopped praying. I thought this was actually quite pious of me. I told my pastor one day, "I'm just going to stop praying for a husband, because obviously God's answer is no. I'm praying and He's not giving me one, which must mean that He doesn't want me to have one—at least not now—so I'm going to pray for other things that I trust He'll answer. I'll pray to be a good daughter, and a better co-worker, and a fabulous aunt. Because, surely, I can see improvement in those areas, where I can't when it comes to the matter of being blessed with a husband."

My pastor, who is always very blunt with me, said, "No. That's a horrible idea." He said, "Consider the father who sits down at the dinner table with his children each night, and he says to them, 'What did you do at school today?' The father knows exactly what his children did at school that day—went to math, learned science, played on the playground—because they do the same thing every day. And he knows what they want for tomorrow in school—chocolate milk and pizza for lunch and a turn at dodgeball in P.E.—because they always want the same things tomorrow at school.

"Your heavenly Father," he continued, "delights to hear your thoughts and your fears and your loves and what's on your mind. It brings Him great joy to hear the desires of your heart. So even if He's not answering in the way in which you think He ought to—and keep in mind that He tells us that His thoughts are not our thoughts and His ways are not our ways—you pray anyway, because He has commanded you to and because He wants you to."

It's so easy to pray, in fact, that Jesus has actually already given us a prayer—the Lord's Prayer:

> [This is] the prayer that He prays for us and the whole world. With this, He gives us His own unique relationship as Son with God the Father and lets us stand in His shoes, joining with Him in His praying. In this prayer, we identify ourselves with Jesus as we pray together with Him for the hallowing of the Father's name and the coming of the Father's kingdom. In this prayer, Jesus also identifies Himself with us and our need for food, forgiveness and protection from temptation. In this prayer, we pray together with Jesus who prays for us and the whole world.[1]

What mercy! That Jesus Himself would identify with us, that He would pray for us! Blessed, indeed, are we.

"You're like a sock," my four-year-old nephew told me nonchalantly one evening at the dinner table, sticking a fork full of chicken into his mouth.

"Excuse me?" I asked.

"You're like a sock," he said again through a mouth filled with mush.

"I don't get it, Jonathan," I said in bewilderment.

"You're like the socks Mom takes out of the dryer that don't have any mate," he said in exasperation, putting his fork down to gesture grandly. "You know, the sock that there's only one of."

Before a smile could even start to spread across my face, he said, "You need to just get married."

Jonathan has always been strangely curious about what it means to be single. Whenever I would stay with my sister and her family for the weekend, he would ask questions such as, "Why do you always go home alone?" and "Why do I only have one uncle but two aunts?"

As a four-year-old, he wanted to understand. As adults, we are only beginning to. But most important, our Father already does. He has given us the gift of speaking to Him in prayer, and so we do. When we can't, when we have no words left or the tears run too quickly to allow us to draw breath, we take comfort in knowing that another is interceding on our behalf: the Holy Spirit.

*So God provides us with His Holy Spirit, not just once
but again and again, whenever we pray. The Spirit
is the Spirit of prayer, for He is not just received by
faith in prayer, but also prompts us when we pray.
Since we do not know how to pray or what to pray
for, the Spirit, says Paul in Rom. 8:26–27, intercedes
for us and in us before God.[2]*

So write their names down on a sticky note. Slap it on your bathroom mirror, and while you brush your teeth, pray for your fellow singles and pray for yourself. On the way to work, in moments of silence at church, as you end your daily devotions, remember before your Father in heaven those for whom the gift of marriage has not yet been given. They and we and, yes, even you, are children loved by God, and that is reason enough to pray.

> Let's be the guys and gals who pray.

✲✲

LIVE IN JOYFUL EXPECTATION OF THE LORD'S BLESSINGS, WHETHER THAT INVOLVES MARRIAGE OR NOT

As singles, one of our greatest temptations is to despair. We pray, and it seems as though we receive no answer. We cry, and our tears yield nothing. We complain to our mothers, and they simply nod and acknowledge our pain. Part of despair is a desire to assume that nothing will ever be right, nothing will ever be good, until we have a boyfriend or until we are married. We put life on hold, waiting until Mr. or Miss Right comes along before we buy a car or take a trip or visit a museum. And suddenly, we are thirty years old, miserable, lonely, sad and carless. We are a pathetic sight to behold.

Instead of waiting for some magical moment to kick-start your life, you can—get this—go ahead and live boldly right now. You are exactly where Christ wants you to be at this moment. His plan for your life is perfect and sure, despite how it may seem to you, and there's a great deal of freedom in this. It means that you can go right ahead and explore that museum, take that hike, try that food, meet that person, drink that coffee, dance at that concert. You're flying solo for now—maybe forever—but your life doesn't have to be gray and gloomy because of it.

(Don't even say it. I already know what you're thinking, because every time I've been given similar advice, I thought it too: "Don't try to make me feel better. Just acknowledge that I'm alone and let me wallow in it!" Well, here's my simple answer: No. So there.)

Your heavenly Father has given you a gigantically huge world filled with ideas and flowers and music and poems and shoes and bugs and battlefields and cafés. They are all there simply to bring you joy. Can you imagine it? Their sole purpose is to work for your good. Music doesn't save lives or invent cures for cancer. But it does perk up your mood or give you a reason to dance around your kitchen while the meatloaf burns. Bugs don't rescue you from burning cars or give you the best haircut you've ever gotten, but they make you marvel at their itty bittiness and wonder at their ability to drag food the size of their torso across the ground. Flowers help the bugs live, but for people they don't do a thing but sit there and look pretty and maybe, on a good day, cause you to smile at their beauty or sniff in their sweet smell.

God has given you all those things simply because He loves you, because He alone is what matters in this life. Boyfriends and girlfriends, husbands and wives all pale in comparison to this: Your heavenly Father loves you in Christ Jesus, and the world—yes, even eternity—is yours because of it.

Make Friends with Others Who Share Your Mutual Values and Beliefs

Let's just clarify: You don't have to date every single person of the opposite gender with whom you come into contact. You can, however, befriend a few of them. Clarification number 2: This means hanging out with couples too, even though there are days when the thought of having to spend time with one more lovey-dovey pair makes you want to retch into your tennis shoes.

The point is this: If you are hanging out in shady clubs where men are feeling you up and other women are dressed as though they forgot the bottom half of their dresses, it's going to be hard to find people who understand, empathize, and support you in what you believe when it comes to theology, morals, and values. So go to those places where you know people like that will be. Get involved in Bible studies. Go to the local brewery's monthly Theology on Tap night. Be in church each Sunday. Join a local young professionals group.

Your friends—married or single—can serve as a tremendous support group for you. Mine did. I have several single friends, and we'd get together each month to get pedicures or enjoy a meal together. Inevitably, the conversation turned to guys and how none of us were dating. There were times when one of us was dating, and the expectations of the other person became a subject of conversation. "How do I tell him I'm a virgin? Is he going to think I'm weird? Worse, is he going to expect me to give that up for him outside of marriage?"

There were other concerns too. "I went too far in my last relationship; what are some good ways for that not to happen again?" "I'm talking to this guy, and I really like him, but I'm not sure who should call whom first."

When these conversations took place, we all knew we were safe. We believed the same things, confessed the same faith, held to the same standards. When one of our friends worried that her new boyfriend might be surprised by her virginity, we rallied around her, reminding her that it was actually something she could be proud of and not ashamed about. When another liked a new guy she'd met, we encouraged her to go to coffee with him and see what he was all about. We supported one another, but mostly, we listened.

That, in no small part, is why it is good to make friends with those who understand you and who believe as you believe. You may be single, but you have a purpose. Sometimes that purpose is to listen to your friends who have spent hours listening to you. You listen because, as a single, you know how hard it is to find someone to listen to you. You don't want to burden your family with your suffering. You feel bad calling your best friend every other night. But with your friends who are in your same boat, you can be open and honest with them, even as they will be open and honest with you.

You choose friends who are aligned with you in the things that matter in this life—in faith, in family—because they won't steer you wrong, and because you won't cause them to step off into the deep end either. Most often, you simply need validation, to be reminded

and encouraged that what you are doing, how you are living, and
the way in which you are waiting (sometimes about as patiently as a
three-year-old who needs into a locked bathroom) is noble and good
and pleasing to your Father. You take a hard right away from the
friends who will encourage you in what your conscience and your
gut tell you is a bad decision: disregarding your sexuality, being
treated by another person in a way that isn't befitting a child of God,
living as though your choices in relationships don't matter or can't
hurt you.

Find good friends, even if it's through blogs and social media.
Whether they live in your apartment building or across the country,
they will be little consciences for you, reminding you of who you are
in your Baptism, that you matter to Christ, and that in their way of
thinking, you're not too shabby either.

Pattern the Relationship of Male to Female as Our Lord Defines These Roles

You may be solo now, but you can already begin to prepare for
the man or woman for whom you are praying. That means behaving
and living in such a way that won't hurt or harm your relationships
in the future and that will teach you already how guys and gals
interact in healthy ways.

A friend of mine dated her future husband for several months
before coming to me with a problem: he hadn't always been Christian, and in the formative years when he wasn't, he'd slept with
more than a handful of women. He'd repented and apologized to
her for it, but it was hard for her to let go. She could imagine it all,
and it didn't help that, as a virgin, she now felt like she was being
compared to the other women in his life.

Another time, I sat through a dinner with my boyfriend's ex-girlfriend where I was forced, for hours, to listen to her extol all his vir-
tues. While all true, hearing them from another woman was hurtful.
He was *my* boyfriend, not hers, and I didn't need to hear that she'd
been in his house or gone to dinner with him or had lunch with his
mom. Objectively, I knew the two of them were over. Subjectively,
I was jealous, angry that she knew things about him that I felt only

I should know. Outwardly, I smiled calmly when she started listing off all the dates they'd gone on together. Inwardly, I had taken off the scarf around my neck and was yanking it around hers. (Hey, I'm no saint.)

Pornography hurts couples too. Another single friend nearly collapsed when her boyfriend told her, "All guys look at porn at some point in their lives. It's not right, but they do." She was devastated. "How can Christian guys *do* that?" she wailed to me. The longer we talked, the more clear her concern became: It wasn't that she was mad at her boyfriend, who admitted to her that he would probably always be tempted by it but hadn't looked at it in years. It's that she now felt as though she couldn't measure up. "If we end up getting married," she said, "I'm never going to be as amazing as those girls."

It doesn't matter that "those girls," as my pastor once told me, are all fakes. They aren't attracted to the people looking at pornography. They aren't their friends. They don't want to go home with them. Their job is to create minimal pleasure for a short while that eventually morphs into extreme pain for an extended amount of time. That's what can be prevented by praying that Christ would enable you to live a godly, faithful life already now: hurt, heartache, and suffering. (Can we all agree we have enough of that already?)

If you are dating, consider that your gal is someone's—perhaps yours, perhaps someone else's—future wife. Treat her as you would want another man to treat your future wife. Are there things from your future wife's past that would make you jealous or frustrated if you were to marry her? Stay away from them. Are there actions that would infuriate you if another man were to do them to her? Don't do those either. Pray for patience and for grace, that you would care for her as Christ cares for His Church, with only good and right and holy things in mind.

If you are a man, pray for the understanding to give. If you are a woman, pray that you would learn to receive. Guys, be bold in caring for the women in your life. Ladies, let the men do it. The world will kick and scream and stomp its foot like a two-year-old, but don't give in to its temper tantrums. It will tell you that men and women are exactly alike and equal in every way. It will convince you that women don't need men and that the single life is the life of choice— not because it allows you to be about the things of God in a more profound way but because it focuses all the attention on *you*.

As my dad used to tell me, "You're not unique." And in a way, you're really not. You live and breathe and work and cry and put your skinny jeans on one pant leg at a time, just like the rest of us. But in another way, you really are unique. You are different, set apart for the purpose for which God created you. You are a humble, self-sacrificing woman who cares for and receives from the man the Lord may give you. You are a strong, faithful man who gives to and protects the woman God may place in your life. You are that woman and that man already, and while you are waiting—perhaps to meet your husband or wife or perhaps to live a life of service to the Church and to Christ—you can already bear witness to Christ.

The culture will tell you that you are outdated and archaic and so forty-two seconds ago. It will tell you you're not liberated and that to really *live* in this world means that you get to do whatever feels good. And if it feels good, it must be right, even if what's right for you isn't what's right for me. But your conscience—that which God binds to our hearts and which innately works within each of us—will tell you different. Your Lord tells you different. The Church does too. God has instilled us in the faith to go about each day as His baptized child: a new creation, full of life and forgiveness and freedom. Who needs fake equality when you can have the tangible stuff instead? And you can. You already do. It's yours in Christ.

Remember that Being Single Is
an Important Vocation

It is, despite the fact that you think I'm writing this to make you feel better or to give you a false sense of self-worth that will hold you over until you meet the perfect woman. (Spoiler alert: There are none. See? I'm *not* just here to make you feel better! I'm here to make you feel *worse*. Wait, that didn't come out right. Hey, come back!)

Vocations are wide and varied. They are the ways in which we love our families and how we care for those in our communities, in our churches, and in the workplace. They are the tools by which our Lord tends to your neighbors down the street who let their dog do his business on your lawn. They are the masks behind which God conceals Himself, the EMTs in the ambulance who take you to the hospital when you didn't slam the brakes hard and fast enough. They are the means by which you heal, the counselors who listen to your unintelligible thoughts and cries over being lonely. That is, through our vocations, God cares and provides for others. Some are given to the vocation of fatherhood and some to the vocation of farmer. Others care for souls as pastors and still others tend to our vehicles as mechanics. We, right now, have the vocation of being single. But we also have the joy of other vocations as well: choir members, unit executives, sisters, cousins—you name it. These aren't unimportant things to sneeze at. They may not be that of husband or wife, girlfriend or boyfriend—the vocations you *really* want—but they are the places God has put you in right now, and that's something.

Conclusion

Consider What's Coming

As singles, we have a leg up on everyone else. We already know how to live and exist in a way that couples don't. And so one of our greatest joys is one we can't even really begin to comprehend quite yet: everyone will be single in heaven. This is great news to us, especially since (1) we already have this "being single" thing down pat (move aside, world!), and (2) we won't care whether we're single or not. We'll be too busy singing, "To Him who sits on the throne and to the Lamb be blessing and honor and glory and might forever and ever!" (Revelation 5:13).

> *We spend a great deal of time and energy mining the depths of the image of marriage as a picture of Christ and His bride the Church (Ephesians 5:22-33), and yet have we ever considered that single people, even more than married people, are a picture of the reality of what our lives will be like in the kingdom to come?[1]*

Marriage and the institution of it are for people of this life and this earth. But singleness is for the saints in Christ and for heaven.

Jesus Himself clues us into this in Matthew 22, in a discussion about a woman who was married multiple times—seven, in fact. (I do not recommend this course of action. See how well having multiple wives worked out for Abraham, David, and Solomon. Spoiler: It didn't.) When asked which man will be her husband in the resurrection, Jesus answers matter-of-factly: "For in the resurrection they neither marry nor are given in marriage, but are like angels in heaven" (v. 30).

It may not seem like much of a consolation at the moment. The last thing we want to hear as single people is that—yay, us!—we're going to be single in heaven too. (Actually, that kind of sounds like an epic bummer, now that you mention it.) But comfort is coming, I promise. Here's the kicker: What we are experiencing now will be made perfect in heaven. What grieves us now will be what gladdens us then. What frustrates us to the point of hitting our steering wheels in anger and cursing God will bend our knees and lift our high doxologies at the resurrection. There, our names really will be "single," and we will be okay with it, even rejoice in it.

Then we will be more ourselves than we are now. Then we will be single—perfectly and wholly so—but so will all those who have lived and died in the faith around us. Then being single will no longer be a topic of conversation that frustrates us ("So, do you have kids?"), nor will it create a division between us and our families ("Your sister called; she wants to know if you want to go to dinner with her and her husband tonight—again"). Instead, it will be just one of our many common grounds, one of the things we share with those who are gathered with us around the Father's throne.

In heaven, the spotlight won't be on us and the areas in which we think we lack. It won't be about the loneliness that moves us to tears as we try to fall asleep or the stabbing pain of seeing a wedding party photographed at a park. It won't be a matter of keeping up with peers when it comes to dating, relationships, marriage, and children. It won't be about us.

Instead, in heaven, the focus will be on Christ. In that, we are already ahead of the game. As singles, we practice the way in which we will be fully focused on Him. That is to say, "Single people are a picture of the life to come where we are devoted exclusively to Christ alone."[2] We already know that we can call upon Christ, especially when our dad won't answer the phone. We already know that

He is with us always, even when we are the fifth wheel. We already know that He is the one who will never leave us, even when we go home every night alone.

We are practicing in part now what we will be about fully in heaven. We are getting little glimpses—today, already—of what it will be like. We are already being gathered "from the ends of the earth to celebrate with all the faithful the marriage feast of the Lamb in His kingdom, which has no end" (*Lutheran Service Book* [Concordia, 2006], p. 161). We have sneak peeks of how we will sing with the angels and the archangels and the whole company of heaven—Grandma, St. Paul, your sister who died while still in the womb. We are seeing how time is spent, how it passes, for the believing who are in Christ.

On the day of the resurrection, time will no longer divide us. The line between eternity and earth won't have to be stepped over only at the Lord's Supper or at the reading of His Word. In the resurrection, the line will no longer exist.

On that day, eternity will be ours. We will be content in our singleness. We will no longer be alone, because we will be with our Bridegroom, with Christ, who showed His Bride, the Church, what it means to love through His death on the cross.

> We are practicing in part now what we will be about fully in heaven.

On that day, we will know what it means to be content and whole, to be free of awful breakups or bad first dates, traumatizing dating Web-site experiences or tempting, lustful thoughts.

On that day, we will never be lonely again. Instead, Christ will draw us to Himself. "Return, O backsliding children," He will tell us, "for I am married to you" (Jeremiah 3:14 NKJV).

On that day, He will show us that He has taken it all on Himself—our tears of loneliness, our jealousy of our friends in relationships, our fear of the future, our bitterness at what feels like His silence—and forgiven us for every piece of it.

On that day, more than any other, you will know that you are loved. You are not alone. You are not defined by being single. No, you are a child of God: whole and perfect, broken no more.

ENDNOTES

Chapter 1

1. Christopher Seifferlein, "Let's Hear It for the Single People," Emmanuel Lutheran Church, Pastor's Newsletter Archives, February 2012, http://emmanueladell.org/plarchives/2012/02.html (accessed March 8, 2014).

2. Matthew Harrison, "Witness: Before God and to the World," *The Lutheran Witness* 129, no. 10 (October 2010), http://blogs.lcms.org/2010/witness-before-god-and-to-the-world-10-2010 (accessed March 8, 2014).

3. U.S. Census Bureau News, "Unmarried and Single Americans Week, Sept. 16-22, 2012," Profile America: Facts for Features (July 31, 2012), http://www.census.gov/newsroom/releases/archives/facts_for_features_special_editions/cb12-ff18.html (accessed March 8, 2014).

4. Jonathan Last, "A Nation of Singles," *The Weekly Standard* no. 13 (December 10, 2012), http://www.weeklystandard.com/articles/nation-singles_664275.html (accessed March 8, 2014).

Chapter 2

1. U.S. Census Bureau News, "Unmarried and Single Americans Week, Sept. 15-21, 2013," Profile America: Facts for Features (July 30, 2013), http://www.census.gov/newsroom/releases/archives/facts_for_features_special_editions/cb13-ff21.html (accessed April 4, 2014).

Chapter 3

1. Gene Edward Veith, "The Family: A Place of Refuge," *For the Life of the World* no. 2 (April 2004): 6.

2. Bo Giertz, "Twenty-Three Theses on the Holy Scriptures, the Woman, and the Office of the Holy Ministry," *The Springfielder*, no. 4 (March 1970): 17.

3. G. H. Smukal, "Love and Obedience," *The Lutheran Witness* 59, no. 9 (September 1940): 306.

4. Dean M. Bell, "With Angels and Archangels: Some Thoughts on Real-Time Worship," *Logia: a Journal of Lutheran Theology* 11, no. 1 (Epiphany 2002): 43. www.logia.org.

5. Bell, "With Angels and Archangels," 43.

6. Kevin Huss, "The Scriptural Relation of Man and Woman; Headship: An Element of the Divine Image," unpublished, 7.

7. Smukal, "Love and Obedience," 306.

8. Martin S. Sommer, "The Place of Women," *The Lutheran Witness* 60, no. 11 (November 1941): 384.

9. Huss, "Scriptural Relation of Man and Woman," 6.

10. David P. Scaer, "The Christian Family in Today's Society Viewed in a Biblical Perspective," *Concordia Theological Quarterly* 54, nos. 2-3 (April-July 1990): 96-97.

Chapter 4

1. Irene Soehren, *Why Love Asks You to Wait* (St. Louis: Concordia, 1964), 8.

2. Excerpts from *Treatises on Marriage and Remarriage* by Tertullian, translated by William LeSaint, copyright 1951 by Newman Press/Paulist Press, Inc., New York/Mahwah, NJ, page 35. Used with permission of Paulist Press. www.paulistpress.com.

3. Tertullian, from *Treatises on Marriage and Remarriage*, 35.

4. Chrysostom, "Homily 19," *On Marriage and Family Life*, trans. Catherine Roth, David Anderson (Crestwood, NY: St. Vladimir's Seminary Press, 1986), 41-42. Used with permission.

5. Chrysostom, "Homily 19," 49.

6. Chrysostom, "Homily 19," 46.

7. Chrysostom, "Homily 19," 46.

8. Ambrose, in *Marriage According to St. Ambrose*, by William Dooley (Baltimore, MD: Catholic University of America Press, 1986), 126.

9. Ambrose, in *Marriage According to St. Ambrose*, 133.

10. Pope John Paul II, "Marriage and Continence Complement Each Other," *L'Osservatore Romano*, Weekly Edition in English, 19 April 1982, page 10, http://www.ewtn.com/ library/papaldoc/jp2tb77.htm (accessed March 21, 2014).

Chapter 5

1. Colleen Carroll Campbell, "Facing Feminism: A Closer Look at Its Discontents," *Salvo*, issue 25 (Summer 2013), http://salvomag.com/new/articles/salvo25/facing-feminism.php (accessed March 10, 2014).

2. Regis Nicoll, "Porn Is Not Free: The High Social & Personal Costs of Pornography," *Salvo*, issue 16 (Spring 2011), http://www.salvomag.com/new/articles/ salvo16/16nicoll.php (accessed March 10, 2014).

3. Donald L. Hilton Jr., "Slave Master: How Pornography Drugs & Changes Your Brain," *Salvo*, issue 13 (Summer 2010), http://www.salvomag.com/new/articles/ salvo13/13hilton.php (accessed March 10, 2014).

4. Hilton Jr., "Slave Master."

5. John Coleman, "Porn in the USA: Examining Our National Addiction," *Salvo*, issue 2 (Spring 2007), http://www.salvomag.com/new/articles/salvo2/2coleman.php (accessed March 10, 2014).

Chapter 6

1. John T. Pless, "The Earthquake in Haiti: Again, the 'Why' Question" *The Lutheran Witness* (January 1, 2010), http://blogs.lcms.org/2010/the-earthquake-in-haiti-again-the-why-question-1-2010 (accessed March 21, 2014).

2. Excerpts from *Treatises on Marriage and Remarriage* by Tertullian, translated by William LeSaint, copyright 1951 by Newman Press/Paulist Press, Inc., New York/ Mahwah, NJ, page 15. Used with permission of Paulist Press. www.paulistpress.com.

3. Tertullian, from *Treatises on Marriage and Remarriage*, 15.

4. Tertullian, from *Treatises on Marriage and Remarriage*, 15.

5. Peter J. Scaer, "The Beauty of Holiness," *For the Life of the World* 8, no. 3 (July 2004): 6.

6. Tertullian, from *Treatises on Marriage and Remarriage*, 15.

7. Gene Edward Veith, "Obsolete or Just Misunderstood?" *The Lutheran Witness* 130, no. 7 (June/July 2011), http://blogs.lcms.org/2011/obsolete-or-just-misunderstood-6-2011 (accessed March 10, 2014).

8. Lauren F. Winner, *Real Sex: The Naked Truth about Chastity* (Grand Rapids, MI: Brazos Press, 2005), 145.

Chapter 7

1. Excerpts from *Treatises on Marriage and Remarriage* by Tertullian, translated by William LeSaint, copyright 1951 by Newman Press/Paulist Press, Inc., New York/ Mahwah, NJ, page 31. Used with permission of Paulist Press. www.paulistpress.com.

2. Roger Sonnenberg, "Searching for Love Online," *The Lutheran Witness* 124, no. 2 (February 2005): 17.

Chapter 8

1. The National Campaign to Prevent Teen and Unplanned Pregnancy, "The DCR Report—Section J: Religiosity and Its Association with Sexual Activity, Childbearing, and Marriage among Young Adults Age 20–29," December 2010, http://thenationalcampaign.org/sites/default/files/resource-primary-download/dcr_sectionj.pdf (accessed April 4, 2014).

2. Thomas Dubay, *And You Are Christ's: The Charism of Virginity and the Celibate Life* (San Francisco, CA: Ignatius Press, 1987), 7.

3. Dubay, *And You Are Christ's*, 12.

4. Dubay, *And You Are Christ's*, 16.

5. Irene Soehren, *Why Love Asks You to Wait* (St. Louis: Concordia, 1964), 11.

6. Soehren, *Why Love Asks You to Wait*, 21.

7. *Lutheran Book of Prayer* (St. Louis: Concordia, 2005), 225.

8. Lauren F. Winner, *Real Sex: The Naked Truth about Chastity* (Grand Rapids, MI: Brazos Press, 2005), chapter 6.

9. Casey E. Copen, Kimberly Daniels, William D. Mosher, "First Premarital Cohabitation in the United States: 2006–2010 National Survey of Family Growth," National Health Statistics Reports, no. 64 (April 4, 2013), http://www.cdc.gov/nchs/data/nhsr/nhsr064.pdf (accessed March 10, 2014).

Chapter 9

1. William Congreve, *The Mourning Bride*, Act III, Scene 8.

Chapter 10

1. Regis Nicoll, "Porn Is Not Free: The High Social & Personal Costs of Pornography," *Salvo*, issue 16 (Spring 2011), http://www.salvomag.com/new/articles/salvo16/16nicoll.php (accessed March 10, 2014).

2. Nicoll, "Porn Is Not Free."

3. "God's Own Child, I Gladly Say It" (*Lutheran Service Book* 594:3), copyright © 1991 Robert E. Voelker. Used by permission.

4. Rev. Jason Braaten, personal e-mail.

Chapter 11

1. John Kleinig, "The Gift of Prayer," *The Lutheran Witness* 131, no. 6 (May 2012), http://blogs.lcms.org/2012/the-gift-of-prayer-5-2012 (accessed March 10, 2014).

2. Kleinig, "The Gift of Prayer."

Conclusion

1. Christopher Seifferlein, "Let's Hear It for the Single People," Emmanuel Lutheran Church, Pastor's Newsletter Archives, February 2012, http://emmanueladell.org/plarchives/2012/02.html (accessed March 8, 2014).

2. Seifferlein, "Let's Hear It for the Single People."

Art Credits

About the Author

Adriane Dorr Heins dated guys, broke up with guys, got broken up with by guys, got engaged to a guy who broke off the engagement then asked her to marry him again then broke off the engagement again (stay with us here), dated a little more, and then finally met and married her husband at the age of 29.

Speaking to and on behalf of singles within the church, she engages various groups and entities within the church about the role of women as well as how to incorporate singles into the life of the Body of Christ. She also answers questions and offers help to singles who connect with her via social media, many of whom ask not for relationship advice but for prayers on how to help their families understand what it means to be single.

A Bachelor of Arts graduate of Concordia University Wisconsin and a Master of Arts in Religion graduate of Concordia Theological Seminary, Adriane served as Associate Executive Director for Strategic Communications for The Lutheran Church—Missouri Synod (LCMS) before marrying her husband, Chris, a dairy farmer in Missouri. She now works deployed as Managing Editor of *The Lutheran Witness*, the LCMS's flagship publication, from a cheery office overlooking eighty Holstein heifers.

Chat with Adriane by following her on Twitter (twitter.com/adrianedorr), Facebook (www.facebook.com/adrianea.dorr), or by following her blog Stet (letitstet.wordpress.com).